A SHOCKINGLY
BECOMING YOUR OWN

MEDIA
WHORE

Daniel Shehori with Steven Shehori

Self-Counsel Press
(a division of)
International Self-Counsel Press Ltd.

Self-Counsel Press acknowledges the financial support of the Government of Canada for our publishing activities. Canada

Printed in Canada.

First edition: 2017

Library and Archives Canada Cataloguing in Publication

Shehori, Daniel, author

Media whore : a shockingly simple guide to becoming your own kick-ass publicist / Daniel Shehori with Steven Shehori.

Issued in print and electronic formats.

ISBN 978-1-77040-295-9 (softcover).—ISBN 978-1-77040-488-5 (EPUB).—ISBN 978-1-77040-489-2 (Kindle)

1. Publicity. I. Shehori, Steven, 1971-, author II. Title.
HM1226.S54 2017   659   C2017-904973-9
                                           C2017-904974-7

Cover design by Kurt Firla (KurtFirla.com)

Self-Counsel Press
(a division of)
International Self-Counsel Press Ltd.

Bellingham, WA   North Vancouver, BC
USA   Canada

CONTENTS

Samples

NOTICE TO READERS

Laws are constantly changing. Every effort is made to keep this publication as current as possible. However, the authors, the publisher, and the vendor of this book make no representations or warranties regarding the outcome or the use to which the information in this book is put and are not assuming any liability for any claims, losses, or damages arising out of the use of this book. The reader should not rely on the author or the publisher of this book for any professional advice. Please be sure that you have the most recent edition.

ACKNOWLEDGMENTS

Thank you very much to the following people and organizations for their guidance, support, and assistance with research: Liana Vieira, Kurt Firla, Ron Tite, Anaiah Shehori, Glenn Sumi, John Pollock, Maryam Siddiqi, Jan Murphy, Linda Richards, Eileen Velthuis, Richard Ouzounian, Kenny Herzog, William Grajeda, and The Second City.

This book is dedicated to Mom, Liana, and my dog. Thank you ladies.

FOREWORD

I grew up with the Shehori brothers.

Not in a the traditional "we were neighbors" or "we were in kindergarten together" kind of way (although I'm sure they were adorable children). We grew up together professionally in Toronto's comedy scene. Whether it was performing in Lucille's Ball at The Oasis, being a part of The Chick 'n' Deli's first ever comedy night, or participating in various sketch and stand-up shows at The Second City's Tim Sims Playhouse, we collaborated on projects, explored characters, wrote scripts, produced plays, and generally found our way developing works of art that we thought were important and groundbreaking.

Some were.

And some certainly were not.

That's what happens in comedy. It takes years to develop your voice. Over time, you try stuff, write stuff, workshop stuff, test stuff, and generally focus on taking the next step in the craft.

The only goal is to deliver a line or a bit that connects with the audience and induces tears of laughter.

But it doesn't work if there's no one there to applaud.

It's the other side of performance that rarely gets talked about. While great artists can spend years developing their painting technique or musical ability or comedic timing, they often disregard the other critical skill needed to make it: Getting bums in seats so that you actually have an audience to perform to. As with the old "if a tree falls in the forest … ," if an artist delivers an amazing show that no one sees, does it still count?

I've always considered publicity to be the performance before the performance, and it's for a completely different audience with different needs and different objectives. You think it's tough connecting with an audience obsessed with the phones in their hands? Try connecting to an entertainment writer on a deadline who has 20 pitches and 35 press releases on his or her desk.

The Shehori Brothers always understood the live audience, but they also worked the publicity audience. Just as comedians take years to develop their craft, the Shehori Brothers rolled up their sleeves, ground it out, and spent years developing their publicity skills through experimentation, trial and error, common sense, and creative brilliance.

Thanks to their generosity, you don't have to do that. Everything they've learned is here in convenient book form.

As they say in these pages, no one can sell you like you can sell you. Your work is far too important and you've spent a lot of time developing it. Don't stop there. Use the brilliance of this book to finish the job. Be your own media whore. Thanks to these guys, it has never been easier.

Enjoy the book. I know I did.

— Ron Tite
Coauthor of *Everyone's an Artist (or At Least They Should Be)* and
CEO of The Tite Group

INTRODUCTION

There was a time I didn't know what a publicist was. I had a vague idea, assuming it was a person you called if you were a celebrity involved in a scandal you believed could only be remedied by some dramatic spin to the media. In some respects, I still don't really know what a publicist does, which is odd given my brother Steven and I have been calling ourselves publicists for many years. So if I'm not entirely sure how to define this mystery profession, what am I suggesting we've been doing this entire time?

I've since learned you can hire a person (a publicist) whose job it is to help you garner media attention for your art/show/sporting event/product/restaurant/book/business — whatever it is you'd like the public to be aware of. Like with all professions, the good ones tend to cost a lot of money.

If money isn't a concern, simply hire a publicist and give this book to a friend. (Unless you're reading this from your tablet — that would be dumb.) Although before you do, ask yourself this question: "How do I know if I'm hiring a good one?" I'm not sure. I've never paid for a publicist, but the good ones must exist. To be honest, I don't even know how the good ones go about it, or the bad ones for that matter. I only know how my brother and I do things, and we've developed a system that's served us — and more importantly, our clients — extraordinary well over the years. In fact, we've nabbed more mainstream media attention than I can begin to remember. Countless newspaper articles, reviews, magazine cover stories, radio interviews, national television spots, and all forms of online press. We've felt grateful and fortunate to have helped new artists, charities, businesses, government organizations, and legends of multiple industries. This book lays out many years of methods discovered and brought about by love, fear, trial, and error.

1. Who and/or What Is a Media Whore?

Who or what is a media whore? Me, I suppose. Would you read a book simply called *How to Get Media Attention*? Perhaps you would. Placing a mildly controversial word in the book's title to garner extra exposure is something I suspect a media whore would do.

In my opinion, the word "media" itself is not controversial. The word is not specific to gender as the word is neutral. I have been taught that every word is neutral until someone gives it meaning. Yet still it seems that this word "media" often has a negative connotation attached to it. Or perhaps, like the word itself, the media is neutral and it is me who has assigned negativity to it.

I constantly judge any news story in three different ways: Positive, negative, or neutral. What is a neutral news story? I would like to tell you that all stories are neutral, even though I don't treat them that way myself. Coverage of a sporting outcome (as long as you are not emotionally invested in the sport) can be considered neutral. If I am in a bar and glance up at the TV to see that Manchester United lost a soccer game to Real Madrid, this isn't positive or negative, as I don't personally care about European soccer. Or North American soccer, for that matter.

A high percentage of news stories from mainstream media outlets tend to land in the negative column, particularly stories from 24-hour news networks. I recall watching a news station in Toronto, one that has been very nice to me and has given me a ton of media attention over the years, so I won't call them out by name. It's not their fault if they report news stories I decide not to like. This station once reported a story about a dog jumping out of the back of a pickup truck and meeting its demise on a highway in California. Twenty-four hours is a lot of time to fill, so I understand sometimes they have to go out of their way to look for such stories when they can't find them locally. I remember thinking "Why are you showing me this?"

Again, the story was neutral regardless of my negative reaction to it. Some people don't care about dogs, never mind a dog in another country they didn't know existed prior to seeing this on TV. (These people are called jerks.)

As I make baseless assumptions about the motives of corporate media and the people that watch it, I may as well also make assumptions about you, the reader of this material. My assumption is that you are reading this because you wish to obtain media attention about something you love.

My actual understanding of what the term "media whore" really means is: *Someone who will go out of their way to get media attention by almost any means necessary.* To many, this is a term you'd apply to a person you felt was behaving in a shallow and selfish manner. Mind you, it doesn't have to mean this at all. If you are indeed reading this material for the purpose of shining a light on something you love, I'd very much encourage you to be shallow and selfish. It is what it is, and love is love. In my biased opinion, the media needs more of your love and fewer unfortunate dog stories. May the following information be easy to comprehend and fun to apply, allowing you to gracefully whore as much love as you can out to the world.

By the way: I know life gets pretty hectic sometimes, which means maybe you've purchased this book and, despite the best of intentions, won't get around to reading the damn thing anytime soon. Or maybe you've read it, yet despite all the magical advice within these equally magical pages, you'd still rather hire a publicist instead of going at it yourself. If that's the case, Steve and I won't object to you hiring us for your next project. (Remember: A publicist who doesn't publicize himself or herself ain't much of a publicist.) Just pop by www.SweatEquity.ca for more info. I'll likely give you a discount, since you bought this book and all. Unless you're a jerk, that is, in which case I'll charge you more. OK, cool — good talk.

CHAPTER ONE

WHY DON'T I JUST HIRE A DAMN PUBLICIST? (OR, WHY DO IT MYSELF?)

If you build it, he will come.

— FIELD OF DREAMS

Remember that line? From the Kevin Costner movie? Pretty inspiring, no? Of course it is. Mind you, if you build it and don't also build the proper relationships to get the word out, it's quite possible the ghost baseball player may not come. Which means you plowed that stupid cornfield for nothing.

Say your friend knows someone you'd like to date. At your behest, he agrees to put in a good word for you. There are no guarantees this will work, but it's worth a shot, and hey, your friend is in a much better position to get the ball rolling than you are.

From my perspective, this is the basic role of the publicist: To take the relationships he or she has forged and apply them on your behalf. Which is a pretty good deal. Of course, unlike your buddy, they're going to charge you for it, while keeping the "no guarantees" clause intact, naturally.

Consider This Idea: So yeah, publicists are wonderful and smart and good looking and so on and so forth. However, when you're passionate about something and want to get the word out, nobody can sell it better than you can. You're the one who has invested all the time, thought, and energy. Which absolutely makes you the ideal person to talk about it with others, yes? Yes, it does.

Maybe you feel your creation isn't yet worthy of media attention. Of course, you've gone through the process of creating it anyway, which strongly suggests it must hold some value. It does. Let's start with this hypothetical example: You and your friends have formed a band. You're new to the scene but are nonetheless excited about what you've put together. Although you want to get your name out there, there's a good chance you're thinking, "Why would the media care about us? They've never heard of us and we haven't done anything noteworthy yet." Why, indeed.

Everyone has a story. Even those new to the game. Because being new to the game means you were doing something completely different up until this point. And guess what? That's a pretty cool story. Is it a story that'll land you a magazine cover? Probably not, but then again you never know. Although it's completely fine if the media doesn't find your origin story all that riveting. This story is just beginning, and there's plenty of time to make it all the more compelling. (Believe me, you may be far more engaging than Steve and I were when we started out.) Because as the person who's most dedicated to your creation, you're far more likely to be consistent and persistent. *Consistent* meaning you intend to do the thing you're doing for a long time. *Persistent* meaning you're intent on building a relationship with the media while you continue to learn and develop what you're doing.

Say you live in New York City and you've got something to promote. There's a decent chance you'll find it daunting to reach out to a major media outlet like *The New York Times*. Again, you may be thinking, "Why would *The New York Times* care about what I'm doing? Nobody's heard of me before." Fair enough. But here's the first thing to remember: It isn't the daunting 166+-year-old entity known as *The New York Times* you're reaching out to. You're reaching out to one singular human being at the other end of a computer/telephone. He or she is not 166 years old, and certainly isn't taking credit for the vast majority of things that made the *Times* a media giant.

Now, your task is a hell of a lot smaller. All you have to do is appeal to this one human being — and if you can convince this one person to give your creation a little bit of coverage, the amazing irony starts. Now you don't just have his or her personal endorsement — you have the endorsement of the daunting 166+-year-old entity known as *The New York Times*. I'll expand on this idea later on but the takeaway for now is pretty clear: Focus on the person, and not where he or she works.

As Steve tells people when we give seminars on this information: "When you're contacting the media, you want to have a little more to your story than 'local rock band to perform rock music at local rock venue.'" This is some fine advice with regards to learning publicity, and really, for your life in general.

To reiterate, even when first starting out on your journey, you're the best person to speak about your thing. A contrary argument to this could be found in the real estate industry. You may love the home you live in, but does this make you the best person to sell it? A beautiful home that's been well maintained with love can likely sell itself — however, we know this isn't always the case. My lack of initial success in obtaining media attention could have suggested we weren't the best people to sell the idea of our projects to the media. Thankfully, in our case, the stakes were much lower than selling a home on the open market. A real estate agent has been trained to pick out the finer details a potential buyer may be looking for — ones you may not have considered. As such, you're still the best person to sell your home as long as you pay attention to many of the finer details — ones that can easily be communicated with others. If you were equipped with this information, you'd have no need for a real estate agent.

Many people sell their own houses without professional help and save a ton of money in the process.

This book is full of fine details for you to consider, and the good news is that since your thing likely doesn't involve a transaction worth hundreds of thousands of dollars, the stakes are considerably lower. It takes 60 to 170 hours of training to become a real estate agent. Meanwhile, you can plow through this book in a sitting or two.

1. Why Trust Us to Teach You How to Be a Media Whore?

As mentioned, Steve and I never intended on becoming publicists. We had no official training in communication studies, and although there are many educational facilities that will teach you how to become a publicist, we never bothered to look into them. Reason being, it was never a long-term goal of ours to learn how to do this. So why would you bother to read a book on a subject written by people who admit to no formal education on the very same subject? (I'm not sure. Maybe because the cover looks cool? I have a tendency to judge books by their covers.) It was never intended as a long-term endeavor; however, it certainly has become one.

In hindsight, had I been aware I was going to spend years doing this type of work, I may have considered looking into some formal training back in the day. I am sure I would have benefited from it. Conversely, the benefit of going about it the way it naturally occurred now illustrates the important foundation of this information. If ignoramuses with a lack of formal knowledge on the subject can find a way to obtain a never-ending stream of media attention for the things they love, then certainly anyone can do it too. That's what makes for the great story behind the cool cover.

CHAPTER TWO

WHAT'S IN IT FOR ME IF I DO IT MYSELF?

As long as you're going to be thinking anyway,
THINK BIG.

— Donald Trump, WWE Hall of Famer

You may be someone who reads this quote and recognizes value in these words. You may also be someone who reads it and thinks, "Did this book really just quote that guy?" Any personal opinions about the man aside, his quote applies nicely to whatever it is you're looking to do. As long as you're thinking about your project, you might as well think big. Objectively, if Donald Trump didn't choose to think big, you'd never have heard of him, and therefore wouldn't hold any opinion of him, positive or otherwise.

Initially, Steve and I learned how to engage the media for the sole purpose of shining a spotlight on our own projects. We were two young, brash upstarts from Canada, trying to make a name in the comedy scene in our lovable, folksy little Canadian town called Toronto: A place known and appreciated across the country for its friendly, welcoming atmosphere. The Halifax of Ontario. Some people even adoringly refer to it as "The Center of the Whole Universe!" Toronto, pronounced "Torronah" by local townsfolk, is probably best known for its inimitable brand of sarcasm. I do my best to illustrate this in written form, however, much as it is with Montreal bagels, it's something best experienced in its *milieu naturel*.

Anyhow, with a population in the neighborhood of 3 million, Toronto is actually a large media market; the largest in Canada and fourth in North America. Not including Mexico of course. Nothing personal against Mexico, I just don't speak Spanish and I'm ignorant to whatever media outlets it may have. So for the purpose of sharing this information, I'm going to pretend Mexico doesn't exist by building a mental wall. (Make no connection between the Trump quote and the mental-wall treatment of Mexicans in this book. *!Gracias!*)

Before building a mental wall, allow this idea to sneak over your mind's border into your subconscious: The information in this book will work with the Mexican media as well. Or the New Zealand media. Or the Azerbaijani media. Even though that last country may be made up, the point is there's a universal quality to all of this. We're going to focus on the person and not where he or she lives.

When Steve and I wrote, directed, and produced our first sketch comedy show back in 1999, we wanted people to see it. We believed that if the media talked about our show, members of the public (a.k.a., not just family and friends) might show up. We were thinking big, and yet we didn't fully realize what thinking big could entail. (Worth noting that you should never rely solely on potential media attention to draw people to your event.) In my city, unless you're the Toronto Maple Leafs, it's nearly impossible to be guaranteed an audience on a regular basis. Although this book primarily focuses on nabbing media attention, the secondary benefit is that it'll help you become more receptive to marketing and producing ideas.

If you're reading this (and clearly you are; otherwise, how would you be reading this?), your wish is for the general public to come experience what you're doing. As an artist, athlete, author, or businessperson of any kind, engaging with the media can and will expand your brand. And yes, I promise to never utter the term "expand your brand" again.

Does thinking big mean visualizing and then seeking large media outlets to cover your thing? Definitely, although there are other benefits worth considering. Think about how attaining newspaper articles or radio and television interviews can play a key role in everything from grants to sponsorships to work visas. The media coverage Steve accrued over the years was a cornerstone of his successful US green card application. (He now lives in Hollywood, where it never snows and there's a guy dressed like Spider-Man on every corner.)

At the risk of sounding like a late-night infomercial: But wait, there's more! Media coverage works as a form of currency to assist you in finding new work, building a deeper client base, signing on with an agent or a manager, attracting business partners and investors, and even securing more coverage. Once the results come in, your rate of success will improve, since you're now in a position to reference your previous media coverage.

The key once more, is to be consistent and persistent. *Consistent* meaning you're continually growing and coming up with new ideas. *Persistent* meaning you're continually presenting these ideas to the media. And being consistent is entirely relative to what you're doing, so don't feel you need to overwork yourself to stay connected to the media. An author may feel writing a new book every six months is consistent. Another author may feel once a year is a better pace. This means the frequency at which they communicate with newspapers, blogs, TV, and radio contacts will vary accordingly. The same rules apply to you: Contact them when you need them, but be consistent. This shows you're someone to be taken seriously.

When Steve and I produced that first sketch show, what we were really gunning for was prepress. So what's that? It's media attention that predates the release of your thing. A blog or newspaper article. A radio, TV, or podcast interview. Even though some reviews can precede official release dates (e.g., movie reviews), I'm not counting those as prepress. Reviews are fantastic — when they're positive — and may be worth seeking. (More on them later.) But obviously, you're rolling the dice. There's no dice rolling with prepress. Since it's not a review, the coverage is pretty much guaranteed to be 100 percent positive. If BuzzFeed, NPR, or a local blogger bestow you with prepress, you're not just getting the word out. You're getting their implicit endorsement. This can be priceless.

How much prepress did we end up getting for our debut hilarious sketch comedy effort? Zero, of course. We were the comedy people staging a comedy event at the local comedy venue. In other words, we did not know how else to phrase it to sound interesting. To be honest, it took us well over a year of being very consistent and persistent before anyone in the Toronto media even responded to us. Sure, it was frustrating at the time, and yet immensely valuable in hindsight. Every so-called failed effort on our behalf validated the success that eventually followed. And since we learned from our failures, you now get to learn from them too.

Naturally, my goal is to spare you from as many of these frustrations as possible. Although keep in mind, there are no failed efforts in the world of publicity, and nothing you do will ever be in vain. In other words, if you're not receiving the desired results right away, it doesn't necessarily mean you're doing anything wrong. Remember: consistent and persistent.

 Consider This Idea: What you're trying to promote is important, but it's never as important as what you'll be promoting next. What does this mean? This means you don't want to give up after a lack of initial results. This means being consistent and persistent, so the momentum and energy from your current project will carry over into what you're doing next. This means you don't want to angrily call out a media contact for not getting back to you, or pressure/guilt him or her into some prepress. This behavior may deter future coverage he or she might eventually have sent your way.

The fact is that media outlets may not always have the time or space to facilitate something for you. The good news is that the more you stay on their radar the more they'll take notice, and the more your relationship will build. They need content. You need promotion. It's a naturally symbiotic relationship.

CHAPTER THREE

ENGAGING THE MEDIA
FOR THE FIRST TIME

If you want some … come get some.

— JOHN CENA, PHD, THUGANOMICS

It never hurts to ask.

— MOM, AS SHE WOULD OFTEN REMIND US

Notice that we've been referring to your beloved creation as your "thing," since we don't know what your thing is. Fortunately, when it comes to the information laid out in this book, it doesn't matter what your thing is. Make sense? Good. Onwards.

Now comes the simple answer to why you're reading this information. The big question: "How do I get media attention?"

You're going to ask for it.

Oh, just like that? Just going to ask the media for coverage and have them magically grant my requests?

Yeah, just like that.

We're not suggesting every time you ask they're going to say yes. Of course not. From project to project it's a small percentage of our overall media list that will respond favorably. Not all of

17

them will be interested in what we're doing. However, because Steve and I have been at this for so long, some of them always will. This in part is what's referred to as the law of averages. We're consistent enough that eventually all the media we seek will be interested in something we're doing. And remember: We're not just seeking media coverage for our current project, we're seeking media coverage for projects yet to be thought of.

1. Who Am I Asking?

You're simply going to seek out members of the media that are amenable to what you're doing. What does that mean? If you're a band, you obviously want people who cover music. Only it isn't always obvious. If your band is contacting your favorite local newspaper, you want to seek out the music editor and/or a specific writer that covers your style of music. If the newspaper doesn't have a music editor, then seek out the arts/entertainment editor. If the paper doesn't have an A&E editor, the next logical step is to move away from the dump of a town you call home. It can no longer contain you. (Kidding, not kidding.)

2. How Do I Seek out People to Ask?

Let's talk web. In the world of publicity, the Internet is your best friend. Picture in your mind's eye your current best friend. Can you visualize that person? Great. Compared to the Internet, he or she is useless.

What makes the web so great for publicists? First off, all media outlets have a website, and that's a big deal in present-day society. If you're reading this information 50 years from the original publishing date, then perhaps you people don't have websites. That's right, I said "you people." I'm a "futurist." In the future, this word might come to mean "someone who's bigoted towards all future humans."

Right, so all of these present-day websites have a contact section. Many of them list the exact person you're looking for, along with a way to reach him or her. If you don't see this information on the site, simply call the phone number provided and ask for the name/email address of the person in the position you seek. They'll give you that information; this isn't some bizarre, out-of-left-field request.

Certain media outlets have more of an open format. For example, talk radio and morning TV news/talk shows. In these instances, you want to seek out the producer (or segment producer) of the show you're looking to reach. Morning TV shows often have more than one producer, which means — yes — you can reach out to them all at once. It's fine, they're used to it. The open format means they don't cover anything too specific. In other words, if you're a hip hop artist, the instinct would be to seek out media that covers this genre of music. I'm suggesting you also seek out general talk shows, which will feature hip hop artists, politicians, chefs, charity organizers, or whoever's doing something interesting.

The term "applicable" comes into play here again. I've been told by editors and producers about the countless irritating email blasts they receive from people trying to promote things completely not in their wheelhouses. Don't be that person. If the thing you're trying to promote is regional, you don't want to contact folks outside your neck of the woods. In other words, if you're putting on a live comedy show in Toronto, don't bother the New York media just because they happen to be on your list. But, if your thing isn't regional and has an online presence (such as a crowdfunding campaign), then by all means reach out to the global media as well as your local outlets.

To reiterate, the theater editor at *The Montreal Gazette* can't assist you with your campaign benefiting clean water initiatives in the Congo. I mean technically yes, this kind soul could help in some way if he or she wanted to; however, this isn't in the job description, so it's best not to bother.

But I thought you said it never hurts to ask?

Shush. If however, you were to write and stage a play in Montreal about this hypothetical water situation in the Congo, the *Gazette's* theater critic is definitely someone worth reaching out to. Also, if you are Canadian and you wrote this play in French, the Canadian government might even rain sponsorship money down on you.

There are businesses online that will sell you comprehensive lists of media outlets around the world, sometimes at a reasonable rate. (We're talking anywhere from hundreds or thousands of names and emails.) These can be valuable if you're in need of calling national or international attention to your thing. I've never used one of these companies myself; otherwise, I'd suggest one. Reason being, you can find this information for free if you're willing to put in the time. Again, your best pal, the Internet, is a blessing when you're first starting out.

Additionally, there are online businesses that can send out your press releases (more on press releases in the next chapters) to as many media outlets as possible. It's a good idea in theory, although we've rarely come across clients who've had much success with this. It's a costly process with few guarantees, and they don't follow up on your behalf. Again, with a little time put into research, you can find everyone you seek without such a service.

If you live in a larger market, it's quite possible you're not even aware of all the media outlets available to you. Simply search online for media in your city/region. Branch out beyond traditional outlets as well. Search for blogs, podcasts, online publications, and student media. You're well aware of the rise of new and independent media available online. There are also many outlets that cater to specific cultural backgrounds and lifestyles. You may be someone who's thinking "But my name is John Straight-Male from White-Bread, Iowa. There's no cultural media outlet specific to me." Of course there is, silly. It's called Fox News. Seriously, though: There's always something.

Steve and I have always been mindful of treating the person from the local school newspaper with the same respect as the editor of a national publication. Aside from abiding to this universal principle of treating everyone as you wish to be treated, there's a practical element at play here. Just like you, the person writing for the school newspaper has larger desires. The consistent and persistent ones move on to the bigger media outlets. The bigger media outlets that you also seek. If you maintain a good relationship with these people, as they excel, so will you.

3. How Do I Ask?

Initially, you should ask via email, and always very nicely. That's intended to sound as simple as I can convey it without coming off as patronizing. Personally, if I felt this was a difficult process I'd have stopped doing this years ago. Sending emails is easy for me. Probably for you as well. To clarify, this "ask" doesn't literally have to be an email. You can use your social media tool of choice for making contact. The point is to not put these people on the spot by calling them on the phone, especially since they don't yet know you. Whenever I engage members of the media for the first time I ask them — via email — how they prefer to be contacted. Every single person prefers email. I'm aware you may have resistance to this, as you may have been taught that if something is important you should pick up the phone. I'm not suggesting you throw that instinct by the wayside, but in the majority of cases it'll serve you well to resist the urge.

 Consider This Idea: People that work in mid- to large-sized media outlets are busy. When you call, you'll likely catch them in the middle of infinite things, and they likely won't have the mindset to focus on you. If they're not expecting a specific call, they likely won't answer the phone at all. As such, I choose to respect the data I've accumulated from surveying these folks, and make first contact via email. There's a time and place for a phone call and we'll follow up with that idea later in a section aptly called "Follow-ups"(Chapter 6, section 1.).

3.1 How busy are these people and why are you telling me this?

My friend Maryam Siddiqi (former Arts Editor of *The National Post*) informed me she would receive on average 100 emails a day for media requests. She would get three to four cold calls a day, and 10 to 15 physical press kits a week. That's a lot of people vying for her attention on a consistent basis. Add all of this to Maryam's regular duties as a writer and editor, and you've got a very busy person on your hands. Personally, I start getting flustered if I have to respond to 10 emails a day.

Here's another example from a regional newspaper. My good pal Jan Murphy is the news/features editor at the *Kingston Whig* newspaper in Kingston, Ontario, Canada (population approximately 124,000). (I have become friends with many people that work in the media over the years, just as anyone does with folks they talk to on a consistent basis.) Despite this relatively small market, Jan receives on average 50 to 75 media requests over email a day, not to mention those trying to get him on the phone.

This information isn't included to deter you from trying, or to make any of this feel daunting. It's to encourage you to a) be nice and b) imagine their perspective the best you can. (Many people never picture the media person's side of things.) In taking the time to do so, you'll naturally engage the media in a kind and respectful tone, just as your parents beat into you as a child. If you're already a nice person, this information may feel self-evident. If you're not a nice person, pretend to be and do this anyway. It will sharpen you into a successful sociopath.

 Consider This Idea: When I'm aware someone in the media is receiving more than 100 emails a day, I strive for my name to elicit a positive reaction when it appears in his or her inbox. It would be very easy for people in his or her shoes to dismiss my contact attempt, particularly if he or she has had a negative experience with me in the past. Even if it turns out he or she is not interested in what I'm doing, my goal is to consistently be an easy, pleasurable person to deal with, one who's always respectful. Again, this is because although what I want to discuss is important to me, it's not as important as what I'll want to discuss next.

The world of sales has driven home the idea that anyone selling something — and publicity is a form of selling — shouldn't take no for an answer. In the world of publicity, the opposite is true. To maintain solid, long-term relationships with your media contacts, respect the "no" and move on, because you'll be approaching them again and again. And how you handle the first no can have a dramatic effect on all the potential yesses that could come down the line.

4. What Exactly Am I Asking For?

What do you want? There are many different ways to be covered by the media, so it's fun and effective to be specific about what you're asking for. Let's take your favorite local newspaper as an example. Your band would love to nab some coverage, but how exactly? If you're familiar with this newspaper, you're probably aware of the different features it offers relative to which field. You've probably come across an interview or a Q & A featuring a band similar to yours in the past. Is this something you'd like for yourself? Ask for it.

I use the band example often because bands tend to perform often. Let's say you've managed to secure your band a weekly gig at a local venue. When you become this consistent, your next step is to assess how often to hail the media's attention. Sending weekly show information to the music listings is a good idea, (more on this later), since it helps reinforce your consistency. That said, you'll want to refrain from asking for media coverage every single week (e.g., an article or interview). Save the big request for when you feel it'll count the most. Examples: A record release party, special charity benefit, or a one-year anniversary of being at the venue.

When pitching your thing, the intent is to create a clear image of it, using words and actual images. A picture says a 1,000 words. That said, a 1,000 words also say a 1,000 words. Fortunately, you won't need a 1,000 words to illustrate your thing in the mind of the person you're speaking with. Start with just one. If you were only allowed to say one word to describe your thing to another person, what would it be? This word will come to you quickly, and it'll be the central theme of the message you build when you contact the media.

4.1 Can you put this all together in a practical and applicable way?

Yep, this can all be put together in a way that works. Once you figure out a) who you want to talk to in the media, and b) what you want to talk about, you're simply going to write a very nice introductory email. There's an example to work from in Sample 1.

This approach works best if you've got the time to send your information to individual members of the media. If you have a very large amount of folks to send your release to, personalize the ones to those you know best and simply send a group email blast to everyone else, with a generic but friendly note at the top that concludes with, "I'll do a quick follow-up down the line. Thank you very much."

Seem simple so far?

Wait a second, Dan, you casually glossed over the words "press release." What the — ?

Hmm, true. Let me pass the baton over to my brother for the next couple of chapters.

INTRODUCTORY EMAIL

Hello Newspaper Editor/Writer, (use his or her actual name, obviously)

My name is John Straight-Male and I'm a part of the rock band "Guilt," who'll be playing rock music at White-Bread's rock venue in a few weeks from now: (*Insert date of performance*).

Below this email (*below, not attached*) is the event's official press release, which includes several story angles I think you could find interesting. The release also includes links to our music, photos, and other pertinent information.

I intend on following up with you in a few days, as I understand and respect how busy someone in your position can be. (*Reminder to make this your own words and feelings, please don't write this stuff verbatim.*) I really liked the article you wrote on that other band from White-Bread that's kind of like us, and I hope to speak with you about potentially doing something similar.

Thank you very much,

JSM from the Bread

CHAPTER FOUR

WRITING YOUR BRILLIANT
PRESS RELEASE

Hey folks — Steve here. Hope the book's been treating you well so far. So let's talk press releases, shall we? Press releases are your primary form of contact with the media. Their function: Call attention to your thing. I've written hundreds of these suckers over the years, and my goal is to spare you the trial and error I went through early on in the process.

First item on the docket: The ol' razzle dazzle. It's imperative your press release is compelling. The reason is obvious: You want — nay, need — to outshine the competition.

Who's the competition? Everyone on the planet looking to promote something who isn't you. The media is inundated with press releases, and as with most scenarios, the cream rises to the top.

The second reason is a tad less obvious, but equally if not more important. Although you should show much-needed respect and reverence to the media, always think of them as ADHD-riddled toddlers.

OK, that's making me sound like a bit of a mean girl, so let's elaborate. As noted a moment ago, the media is inundated with press releases. As Dan mentioned, any given editor, journalist, blogger, or producer can find a metric ton of them swimming around their inboxes each day.

PRESS RELEASE

(1) (2) For immediate release – March 4, 2016

**(3) Award-winning comedians Lisa Schwartzman and Steven Shehori
celebrate episode 50 of their genre-bending podcast...**
(4)

(5) (LOS ANGELES / TORONTO — March 4, 2016) (6) For those who love comedy podcasts but
don't have a couple of hours per week to commit to each one, there's a solution at hand.
Lisa Schwartzman (*Best! Movies! Ever!, Video On Trial*) and three-time Canadian Comedy Award
winner Steven Shehori (Just For Laughs, The Onion's *A.V. Club, The Huffington Post*) are
celebrating their milestone 50th episode of one of the world's shortest podcasts: *You Better
DON'T! is* a riotous weekly seven-minute audio spectacle that comes in like a lion and then quickly
shows itself the door.

Click here for episode 50, *entitled Vegetation Domination,*
where Lisa and Steven get pissed off at plants.

(7) Now 50 episodes in, *You Better DON'T! has* amassed a growing following with Lisa and
Steven's sharp-witted banter and occasionally not-safe-for-work musings. **(8)** "It's part storytelling,
part stand-up, and totally unscripted," Steven says. "We basically just press the record
button, have no idea what we're going to talk about, then suddenly we're discussing Russian tree-
fighting or Paula Abdul's rapping cartoon cat."

The duo's exchanges run the gamut, from pop culture (annoying cover bands, Steven's contempt
for soccer) to personal stories (mortifying romantic encounters, sociopathic grandfathers), to the
plain ol' surreal (vampire lifeguard movies, Super-ball bacteria). Oh, and plenty of squabbling: Lisa
and Steven epitomize the combative brother/sister-style relationship, hilariously tearing each other
down when they're not building each other up.

"We're so comfortable together that we say terrible things to each other with love and impunity,"
Lisa explains. "So a little while back we thought, 'This is pretty entertaining — maybe it's time to
share it with the universe and make tens of dollars in the process.'" The podcast became a reality
after Steven's recent move from Toronto to Los Angeles to write for **(9) The Huffington Post** and
The Onion's AV Club. "The audio is so intimate it sounds like we're in a room together, but we're
actually speaking from different coasts and different countries," Steven reveals. "This podcast has
definitely ensured we'll never lose touch — the poor girl is pretty much stuck with me forever now."

(10) Click on the image below for a 3-minute sample
Click on the You Better DON'T! page for full episodes
Click on the Imgur page for downloadable pics

(11) *You Better DON'T!*
A weekly 7-minute comedy podcast at www.YouBetterDont.com
Subscribe on iTunes, Stitcher, and Tunein

(12) *For interviews or additional information, please contact:*
Daniel Shehori at Sweat Equity Publicity – (phone number here) (email address here)

(13) Hello, this is Lisa Schwartzman's Bio: Lisa has written for, hosted, or video edited over 2,000 hours of television, including HBO, The Discovery Channel, and Showtime. She began her career being chased by a gang of teen neo-Nazis while writing for *The Moscow Times*, *Moscow News*, and *Marketing Russia*. (True story: she got away by making them laugh.) Lisa has performed on-air comedy for CBC Radio, Star TV, and MTV Canada.

Greetings, this is Steven Shehori's Bio: Steven (@stevenshehori) is a TV comedy writer and stand-up comic, a 3-time Gemini Award loser, and a 2-time Canadian Comedy Award winner. He's actually been nominated for 12 Canadian Comedy Awards, so he's happy he finally won a couple, dammit. He's a writer for *The A.V. Club*, *Splitsider*, and the Pulitzer Prize-winning *Huffington Post*, specializing in comedy pieces and celebrity interviews. After 8 years as a senior news and comedy writer for *Naked News*, Steven served as a senior comedy writer for *George Stroumboulopoulos Tonight*, *22 Minutes*, some sitcoms you haven't heard of, and 11 national award shows. Along with his brother Daniel, Steven was a producer for Just For Laughs' *Sarah Silverman & Friends*, featuring comedy legends Sarah Silverman, Louis CK, and David Cross. To boot, their critically acclaimed *Stephen Harper: The Musical!* became the first stage play ever produced at Just for Laughs. This quote from slickrick68 speaks volumes about Steven: "Great eBayer! Lightning fast payment! Would recommend! A+++++++++."

You read right. That's NINE plusses.

(14) (15)

Early in my publicity career, I assumed if I took the time to write a press release, its intended recipients would take the time to read it. The bad news: This belief was laughably untrue. The good news (for you): You're going to learn how to seriously stack the deck in your favor, thereby making your release stand out over much of the competition.

Simply put, media folks end up acting like ADHD-riddled toddlers not because they're flaky and easily distracted, but because for the sake of their productivity (and sanity), they need to sort through information fast. To do so, they're always looking for a reason to discard what's sent their way. If a press release comes off as boring, generic, unprofessional, or too damn lengthy, chances are it's ending up in the delete bin next to those "40 percent off Cialis!" offers.

From years working in the industry, I've concluded there are 15 components to a compelling press release. For your convenience, I've numbered them throughout the sample. (Sample 2 is an actual press release we sent out promoting my charming-as-hell podcast, *You Better DON'T!*) Have a read, and then we'll go over these components step by step. (Don't include these numbers if you work off this template, by the way.)

OK, let's break this press release down piece by piece:

1. The font: Stick with 11- or 12-point Arial for the text. Or at the very least, something that looks Arial-ish. Yeah, Arial is hella lame, but using it shows you're aware of the industry standard. (Ever try submitting a screenplay that didn't use a 12-point Courier font? Bad, bad idea.)

2. The notification: "For Immediate Release" with the date the release is being sent.

3. The tease/set-up: An optional line that comes before your title. This should be concise, informative, and blend seamlessly into what it's teasing, which is in this case, "unscripted musings from comedians Lisa Schwartzman and Steven Shehori."

4. The title: The name of your thing. This is the one exception to the rule re: point size and font. It can — and should — be larger. And steer clear of Arial. Check out Dafont.com for some sweet font options. If possible, make your heading an image. Images are cool. (Don't we look badass as cartoon characters? I paid some dude like $100 to do that for me.) Choose landscape over portrait for your image though (a.k.a., horizontal orientation instead of vertical), so the reader doesn't have to scroll down forever to get to the rest of the text.

5. The dateline: This leads off your opening paragraph and lets the media know where the big event is taking place. Although normally this would be one city, in this instance it's two, given my podcast has a home in Los Angeles and Toronto. The date listed in the dateline corresponds to the date the press release goes out.

6. The opening paragraph: This provides the date, location, and most of the main details. Make it strong, because if it doesn't hook the readers, they won't be moving on to paragraph two. Find the angles that make it unique. If you can't find an angle in your show, either you're not looking hard enough or your show is awful. And trust us, your show isn't awful. You know the old journalism expression, "Don't bury the lede?" This is the lede.

Let's talk tone for a second. And this applies to the entire press release, not just paragraph one. A common mistake people make is to think of their press release as an advertisement. Sure, in a very real sense it is, but the key is not to package it as such. In other words, don't be a carnival barker. Which means avoiding superlatives (e.g., "This event will blow your mind!" or "Prepare to witness the show to end all shows!") Be cool, man. Be cool. That said, you don't have to write in a dispassionate journalism style. The sweet spot is somewhere in the middle. Engage with the media by conveying information in a clear, concise, and accurate manner, while not shying away from selling them on why they'll want to cover it.

7. The body paragraphs: More info. Don't have too many paragraphs in your release, or it turns into homework for the reader. Paragraph one is the most important. Then paragraph two. Then three, etc. Concise. Not esoteric. Provide additional angles, if possible.

8. Quotes: These aren't quotes from the media and/or high-profile entertainment industry professionals; although by all means, add a couple of those in if they'll help your cause. Nope, these are quotes given by either you or someone else involved with your thing. In my experience, a press release without quotes is a dumb press release. Why? Because here's the deal: The media doesn't always have time to set up an interview with you. So quotes are the next best thing. They'll pluck them straight out of the release, add them to their story, and there you have it: instant interview. And the bonus is that you'll sound in-credibly erudite and insightful, since you've painstakingly crafted these quotes ahead of time, as opposed to spew-ing out some nonsense on the spot. (Don't worry, we've got some solid interview tips laid out later in the book.)

Not to keep falling back on the C-word, but keep your quotes *concise*, and don't inundate the release with 'em. A good rule of thumb is two or three. Not sure what to say? Here are a few self-interview questions to start things off:

"The reason I decided to do (my thing) is because … "

"I hope people will get (this benefit) from (my thing)."

"What hopefully makes (my thing) unique is … "

You get the idea. Quotes are yet another place to hit home your angles and show the world why your thing is worth covering.

9. Highlighted words (optional): We alternate on this. Pro: It makes the important info really pop. Con: The media contact looking at it might think, "My brain can emphasize words on its own, thank you very much!"

10. The link(s): If possible, provide a short URL for videos, photos, or something else. The media doesn't want to do a Google search to see if you're good, so samples are very helpful. In this instance, I provide a link to three things:

    A sample clip. Not every press release needs one (it all depends on what you're promoting), but these can be an invaluable way to show your goods, so to speak. In this instance, I uploaded a brief clip to YouTube, then captured an image of the video being played, which I subsequently stuck into the release. When using services like MailChimp (more on that shortly), I can embed a link into the image, so clicking on it will take the reader to the YouTube page and play the video.

    The associated website, which is pretty self-explanatory. If you don't have — or don't need — a website, disregard.

    A link to an Imgur page for high-resolution photo options. This is strongly recommended. If the media doesn't have to email you to track down promotional images, they're more likely to cover your "thing." Imgur pages are free, and allow you to assign vital info to each image.

11. The recap: This is your one-stop shop for laying out and recapping the nitty-gritty details. Simply add all that applies: name, location, time, cost, where/how to purchase, etc. Be sure to bold this info, 'cause it's important.

12. The contact person: If the media wants additional information, they'll likely just hit "reply" on the email you sent. But it's good form to add your contact details to the bottom of the press release, including a phone number,

if possible. If you're publicizing your own show, it's fine to put your own name here. Don't feel like you have to make up a phony publicist pseudonym. Although if you do, might I suggest Dimitri Reginald McCool?

13. The bio page (optional): Bios are splendid, but don't have them gunking up the main body of the press release. They blow the flow, man, so leave them to the end, and keep them taut. Include photos if you'd like, to break up the text.

14. The logo (optional): A logo detailing your thing or its venue can appear at the bottom. Not mandatory, but if you've got one and it doesn't suck, place it at the very bottom.

15. The grammar, spelling, and syntax: This should never be an afterthought. Proofread, proofread, proofread. If you're not a strong writer, get a friend to either write or edit your release. Trust me, you can find somebody. As noted, media folks are always looking for an excuse to stop reading a press release. Skimping on any of these things will reek of unprofessionalism, and into the delete bin you'll go.

By the way, some folks tend to end a press release with "###" or "-30-," one theory is that these are vestigial holdovers from the days of faxing press releases. They're essentially there to indicate this is the end of the document, and there isn't some extra page your fax machine forgot to spit out. With the advent of email, this isn't really a concern. But hey, whatever, add it to the end if it makes you feel funky.

And that's it. You're ready to send this thing! Well, almost ...

CHAPTER FIVE

THE BIG SEND-OFF

Reread Chapter 4. I put a lot of damn work into it.

— STEVEN SHEHORI

Now that you're done and ready to hit "send" to your list of contacts, there are two more small-but-vital steps.

1. Step One: The Sending Part

Your press release will be sent almost exclusively by email. The aforementioned faxing isn't an option. Why? Here's my own spin on a tech joke that's been making the rounds:

MEDIA: Can you fax it to me?

PUBLICIST: Unfortunately I can't, due to my location.

MEDIA: What's your location?

PUBLICIST: The twenty-first century.

You get the gist. Times change, and practices dating back even a short time can become obsolete. One example: For years, we'd email press releases as PDF attachments, to preserve their formatting. These days, that's ill-advised, since emails with attachments are far less likely to be opened due to viruses and whatnot. To boot, text-only press releases listed in the body of an email are duller than a 12-hour C-SPAN marathon.

Another reason we ditched the PDFs? The advent of free email marketing services such as MailChimp, Zoho, or SendinBlue. Not only can you easily create gorgeous-looking press releases on these sites, they'll a) remain properly formatted in the body of your email, and, here's the kicker, b) won't show up as attachments. It's a win-win. Actually, let's add a couple more letters for the hell of it: c) they create a copy of the release online, should you wish to share the URL on social media (rarely a bad idea), and d) they allow you to compile and edit an ongoing, online mailing list of email contacts.

This email marketing option isn't a suggestion, by the way: Definitely use one of these services, lest you look like a serious goober.

Are you a visual learner? They typically have instructional videos on their sites, as well as YouTube. No excuses: Friends don't let friends send PDF or text-only press releases.

2. Step Two: The Email Subject Heading

Imagine you follow each of the steps in Chapter 4 to the letter. You've got a pitch-perfect, fine-tuned press release that's optimally constructed to garner maximum attention. You then send it in an email wrapped in a lame or an ambiguous subject heading. You know, like "Press Release," or "Upcoming Show," or some such rigmarole.

No es bueno. The email's not going to be opened, and all your hard work is for naught. So let's avoid this nightmare scenario courtesy of a strong, well-oiled subject heading. Here are some headings I've written over the years, starting with the one I used to promote the press release we just finished deconstructing.

- Award-Winning Comedians Lisa Schwartzman and Steven Shehori Celebrate Episode 50 of Their Genre-Bending Comedy Podcast

- Vivian Chong Stares Down Blindness in This Candid and Funny True-Life Tale of Determination

- Paul Feig Turns To Viewers To Save His Critically Acclaimed Sci-Fi Sitcom *Other Space*

- Crowdfunding Effort Seeks To Ensure Pillow Fight League's Triumphant Return

- WWE Superstar Chris Jericho Brings His No-Holds-Barred Podcast To Toronto

- Plus-sized Entrepreneur Proudly Opens A One-Of-A-Kind New Fitness Studio For The Rest Of Us

- The Second City's Leslie Seiler and "Superstore's" Lauren Ash Are Here to Turn Christmas Sketch Revues on Their Yuletide Heads

- 40-Year-Old Furniture Mover Releases Stunning Debut Alt-Pop Single

- Hollywood Fugitives Randy & Evi Quaid Pay Surprise Visit to Toronto Fringe Festival Hit

Yes, they're longer than the typical email subject heading (although be sure not to write a novella), but a press release isn't a typical email. The subject heading's goal is to entice your media contact to open up the damn email. You want to pique his or her interest, without going completely over the top. (Again, don't be a carnival barker.)

That's it. One more proofread for good measure, and you're good to go. Which brings us to the next bit of fun: When exactly do you want to pull the trigger on your press release? Let's turn things back over to Dan, he's got you covered.

CHAPTER SIX

WHEN IS THE RIGHT TIME
TO SEND THE PRESS RELEASE?

You may have read news stories about someone like Will Smith signing on to a movie that won't come out for close to two years. This means a press release was sent a couple of years before the actual product was released. That's some serious foresight. Fortunately, Will Smith already has a machine behind him, so it's no big deal. Meanwhile, you have you. For now. I mean you'll always have you, and eventually you may even have your own machine. (Unless those Future idiots have ruined everything for everyone — and the machines have you.)

The point is, you'll want to determine the right time to send out your press release. And there isn't always an exact formula to follow. If you have all the information three months prior to your thing's release, then send it. If you don't have all the information until a week out (tsk tsk), send it. Obviously the more time the better when it comes to generating the best results. In some cases, you may have all the information six months to a year in advance. You're not always expecting coverage a year out, yet depending on what you're promoting, this notice may be warranted.

For example, if you're planning on opening White-Bread's very first transgender bar in one year's time, the good people of W-B may appreciate the advance notice, given such a story could generate some serious pre-buzz. If you're the owner of this hypothetical establishment, such buzz could help attract potential investors, sponsors, and even employees. A potential investor you've never heard of may hear you on the radio and contact you directly. A local beer rep may read about your establishment and jump on the opportunity to help promote your establishment. Potential service staff may eagerly seek you out, without you having to place a "Help Wanted" sign in the window. (Do people still do that?) They'll all come to you directly if you allow them to. The *Field of Dreams* thing again.

In other instances, you may have something big planned in six months' time, but are still a bit short on information. For example, it's December, and you're scheduling a music festival for the following summer. You have the date, venue, and charity info lined up, but you don't yet have all the acts confirmed. In this instance, feel free to send a "Save the Date"-type email giving the media a heads up of what's to come. (Yep, it doesn't even have to be a full-on press release.) The email would simply include the information you've compiled so far, with a promise to follow up with the official press release at a later date. Just like you, the editor of the music section may be planning ahead, and is already working on a summer concert guide.

… So a drunk guy walks into White-Bread's first transgender night club, Unfiltered, owned and operated by Hannah Sanchez (formerly Fil Sanchez). Ms. Sanchez, following the publicity suggestions provided in this book, has now found her business to be booming; so much so that the crowd is at capacity. Having grown impatient at the amount of time needed to be served, the drunk shouts, in a crass manner, "Being that this is my first time in this type of environment, I'm unclear as to who I am supposed to #@!* to get a drink around here!" Unfazed by his outburst, Ms. Sanchez smiles and says, "Excuse me, Sir, please watch your language. This is a family establishment."

Despite her calm demeanor, Ms. Sanchez could have prevented this verbal altercation. How? By having specified in her wildly successful preopening press release that Unfiltered was, in fact, a family establishment, where salty language was strictly frowned upon. An ounce of prevention, you see. So yeah, when you get the information out early, the only surprises that come your way are likely to be good ones.

1. Follow-ups

If you have the luxury of time and you've been able to send your information out several weeks in advance, guess what? You also have the luxury of being patient. You may have been very clever and clear with your press release and introduction, so much so that you've garnered a quick response from media without having to follow up. May this be the case for you often. Oftentimes, it won't be, and that's OK.

Let's say you have six to eight weeks before your band launches its new album. Keeping in mind about how busy you already know these people are, you want to be patient and respectful. If I had this much time to work with, I'd wait at least three to four days after I've sent out the press release before I began following up individually. As in, I'm not following up in a mass email the way I may have done with the initial send-out. This time it's personal. This time I'm addressing individual members of the media with specific ideas or requests. This time — as with every time — I'm being patient and respectful. Similar to how you may not resonate with a person you just started dating who becomes clingy fast. You don't want to point out to him or her that "it's been three days and I haven't heard back from you … " You do wish to point out that you're still very interested in talking to this person when it's best suited for him or her. You do wish to point any additional story angles you may have thought of. Your goal is to simply remain on his or her radar and continue to provoke a positive reaction when your name appears in his or her inbox.

Mentioned earlier was the idea that the phone isn't the initial preferred method of contact. If you still feel you're a more effective verbal communicator, feel free to request a phone conversation at this point. Again, best to ask first instead of just calling.

Ask the media contact if he or she has have time in the coming days for a quick phone conversation. Explain that you feel you can really get across over the phone what you wish to discuss, with both brevity and clarity. Asking for a phone conversation gives the person a space in time when he or she will be focused on you alone. Bonus: This allows you some sweet preparation time, which can be invaluable.

2. What If I Still Don't Hear Back? How Many Follow-ups Is Too Many?

You're not always going to hear back from everyone. It's just how it goes. We've pointed out the high volume of requests people in the media receive. It isn't personal, unless of course you've been impatient and unprofessional with them, in which case it very well may be personal. Most often I don't follow up more than twice. From the initial press release send-out up to the second follow up, this person has now been contacted three times regarding this subject, which means it's time to leave it.

Are you giving up? I don't see it this way, as I'm always going to have something new to discuss with them soon after. I may let this particular subject go with a specific member of the media, trusting that the law of averages will work in my favor and other folks will still be interested.

I emphasize being patient and understanding, yet I'm not always either of those things. When I've become very excited about a project and sincerely believe it should garner attention, and for whatever reason it doesn't, I sometimes get angry and find myself taking things personally. Like a brat. A brat who wants attention and isn't getting it. Fortunately, I keep these sentiments to myself. (Except when I'm sharing them in a book, apparently.)

3. Note about Pitching Cover Stories

If you live in a relatively large cultural center, your city may have one or more weekly arts/culture magazines. I've found these outlets often decide on their cover six to eight weeks in advance. Daily newspapers typically don't require as much notice for a cover story, but again it's best to send the info early if you have it.

Steve and I have felt fortunate and grateful to receive several cover stories without asking. I classify a cover story as being the top story of the section of a particular newspaper/magazine. It can also be the very front of the publication. Although I believe in everything we put forth on behalf of clients, I rarely ask for a cover story unless I truly believe in my heart that what we're doing is worthy of such prestige. That's just me. Maybe I'd get more if I asked more. That said, maybe it would become annoying to the people I'm asking and devalue the next project. Maybe it's not worth overthinking. At the end of the day, I'm grateful for all coverage we receive, regardless of the size.

Objectively I really love all of our ideas. How does one be objective about his or her own creations? Many creators believe that they're not the actual creators, meaning they're more like a creative archaeologist and their thing is just there to be found. Think of it as the statue always being inside the marble before it's chiseled out. The fact that it's already there doesn't make it any less yours; it's simply meant for you to find.

In 2006, Steve and I stumbled across another one of our creations that was just there for us. We discovered our friend Brian Froud is amazingly talented. And with that discovery, we immediately needed to exploit him to further our own careers. (It's OK, he was fine with it.) Brian is one of those freak master impersonators. This led to us stumbling upon his ability to near-perfectly impersonate the characters from Seth MacFarlane's *Family Guy* cartoon. This was a solid jumping-off point, but we needed a way to frame these talents into something new and different. A couple of brainstorming sessions later, we tossed the old public domain novel *Swiss Family Robinson* into the mix and voila! A one-man show called *Swiss Family Guy Robinson*. Our own original idea!

Yes, clearly not the most original idea, but we didn't let that stop us from treating it like it was. Essentially, it was a bastardized retelling of *Swiss Family Robinson*, with a couple dozen *Family Guy* characters replacing whoever the hell was in the novel. It wasn't high theater, but we knew we'd have a hit if we committed to the project and did our due diligence. Upon its acceptance in the Toronto Fringe Festival, we flew in a director from Albuquerque, New Mexico; our friend Mark Chavez, a.k.a., one half of the world-renowned comedic theater duo Pajama Men. Mark has the physical comedy brilliance to make performers look like they're cartoon characters brought to life on stage, which is exactly how we wanted Brian to come across. It simply wasn't enough to showcase a guy in front of a mic doing *Family Guy* impressions while stealing story beats from a book I never read. We wanted this to be the greatest spec script anyone has ever seen, frenetically acted out by a human cartoon character.

Note about flying in Mark Chavez: At that time I was working with the Diesel Playhouse in Toronto, which was gearing up for a major production called *Evil Dead: The Musical* (a show that killed, and continues to succeed all over the world). *Evil Dead* was a few months behind schedule from the original planned opening date, so the venue owner and producers needed something good and quick to have in place in the meantime. I wanted to help, so I went to the good people in charge and said "Hey, why don't you fly in Pajama Men? There are only two of them and they don't require a set or any lighting!"

Pajama Men already had a strong following in Toronto so although I was being all Machiavellian about this, it was still a good suggestion for quality and economic reasons. Mark was hand delivered to us, made some sweet coin from Diesel Playhouse and some meager coin from us, and could rehearse with Brian during the day while performing with Pajama Men at night. A win-win indeed. Thank you, Diesel Playhouse.

For a one-person-show in a big festival, we did very well: stellar reviews, sold-out performances — the whole nine yards. Using our own publicity techniques, we generated a substantial amount of prepress — particularly for a festival show — and were subsequently asked to stage *Swiss Family Guy Robinson* in the

Big Apple itself: Rochester, New York. (OK, the Small-to-Medium Apple. Whatever, man.)

We had every reason to believe our production had all that was needed to become a successful, long-term touring show, akin to such hits as Rick Miller's *MacHomer* and *One-Man Star Wars Trilogy* by the great Charles Ross. However, Fox (owner of *Family Guy*), as they sometimes do, thought differently than we did. We received a cease and desist letter from their lawyers telling us, well, you know, to cease and desist. Ha! Do you honestly think legal jargon written by some unnamed corporate suits from another country could stop our creation? Yes, yes it did.

And yes, there's a point to this long-yet-fascinating tale. Before shutting down *Swiss Family Guy Robinson*, we managed to nab a fantastic cover story about the show's demise from one of Canada's national newspapers, *Toronto Star*. And all it took was Steve writing up a press release about the situation, and sending it to news outlets we thought might find it intriguing. The end result: Several members of the North American media actually went to bat for us in an attempt to help save the show. This included veteran *Toronto Sun* columnist Jim Slotek, who interviewed *Family Guy* creator Seth MacFarlane about it. MacFarlane, to his credit, said "I never saw (*Swiss Family Guy Robinson*), but I did make a call to Fox to say, 'For what it's worth, my two cents, I think you just oughta let the guy do it. I just feel in this day and age with the Internet, because of the enormous exchange of information, intellectual property in some weird way feels public. I just don't see how anything like that hurts the studio.'"

Thank you, Mr. MacFarlane.

You can still find a version of *Swiss Family Guy Robinson* on YouTube, along with other great impression work from Brian Froud (who now enjoys a lucrative voiceover career in animation). Could we have fought harder on trying to bring the show back? Possibly. But as important as *Swiss Family Guy Robinson* was to us at the time, it wasn't as important as what we'd do next.

In 2008, a good friend and excellent actor, Marco Timpano, along with Steve and I, wrote and directed a one-woman show. It was called *One-Woman Show*. Marco played this one woman. To provide some context, Marco didn't dress, talk, or even move like a woman. We made the choice to have him look like an average dude and speak in his normal manly Canadian-from-Italian-descent accent. *One-Woman Show* was the story of a woman tired of being typecast, and continuously auditioning for weak-minded roles. She takes it upon herself to forge her career by creating her own characters to perform.

I loved *One-Woman Show*. In fact, I loved it so much that I wanted it to be a cover story upon its release. So I asked for it. Since I was seeking coverage on a production I perceived to be a big thing I asked to speak with an editor, in person. *One-Woman Show* was entered into a Toronto theater festival (The Fringe; once again) and *Eye Weekly* (RIP), a former weekly Toronto-based Arts/Entertainment magazine, was the festival's media sponsor. The editor of *Eye* at the time, Damien Rogers, benevolently accepted to meet me in person to allow me to state my case for the cover of *Eye Weekly*. She then graciously allowed us to share the cover with one other show. I was very happy about this. I'm still very happy about this. I don't even remember what I said to convince her. I just remember we sat in a park on a beautiful late spring day near the *Eye* office. Mostly, she could sense my enthusiasm for the project, and knew from our professional relationship that I wasn't one to make such a request lightly. Thank you, Damien.

4. Thank You

Express gratitude to the people you reach out to. I know you're aware of this already, so forgive me for pointing it out. You may be hyper-aware of the gratitude movement that has emerged within various religious and spiritual communities. There are many books written within these cultures, specifically on the power of the attitude of gratitude. I haven't read these books myself, but I'm nonetheless grateful that they exist, as I feel I understand the gist of their sentiment based on the description written on their back covers.

Gratitude is sometimes forgetfully laid aside in this busy, vibrant world we live in. Especially when we're not communicating with these people face to face. It's a secondary language unto itself; one whose vocabulary can weaken if it's not used often enough.

I'm in sync with my gratitude, as I'm certain I'd be living in the streets or worse without the kindness, love, and patience of the people in my world. I've become rather OCD about it, to the point that it's never "thanks" and always "thank you," since I don't want to abbreviate my appreciation for others.

Consider This Idea: When it comes to follow-ups, remember to say thank you. I thank the people I contact, in advance, for hearing me out. If a major publication agrees to interview me about my thing, I obviously thank them. I follow up and thank the very same people after the interview has been printed. I thank the writer, the editor, the photographer, the art department, whomever I am aware of that took part in making this happen. I will thank Steve for writing the press release even if it is about him. This applies to interviews about my thing, or any interview I set up for another person. Even if the specific person in the media can't help me, I'll thank him or her for getting back to me. Again, I'm well aware how busy people are, so I sincerely appreciate their time.

I've made a career of being grateful in both my publicity work and creative endeavors, so I feel this topic is well worth mentioning. Thank you very much!

CHAPTER SEVEN

WHAT'S A PRESS KIT?

Traditionally, a press kit is a physical unit that contains outdated clutter (e.g., discs, photo sheets, glossy paper with words) about your thing, that you don't need in the twenty-first century.

So do I need a press kit?

No, but for those who decide it's worth their time, a press kit, whether physical or electronic, would include:

- The press release.

- High-resolution photos. (If you don't know what high resolution means, ask the person taking your photos.)

- Audio/Video of the product, if possible, (e.g., music CD, footage of a performance).

- The product itself, if possible, (e.g., books, app, dog treat).

- Short biography about the creators.

If you've never written a bio before, worry not, as there's no need to overthink it. Look at the bios provided in Chapter 4, Sample 2, and on the back of this book. Ignore the words we made up to sound cool and focus on the simple structure. If you're not sure what to write about yourself, ask someone you respect to write it for you. Ask the person to pretend he or she is you. He or she will fondly highlight points you may be too modest to consider.

A press kit can also include a clever gimmick element pertaining to what you're doing.

A few years back, we offered our media services to some friends staging a comedic play in Toronto. A show I loved called *Jimmy & Vito*. *J & V* was a two-hander about best friends/roommates and the adventures they'd fall into. Jimmy was Greek, and Vito was Italian. Despite the vast cultural differences between Greeks and Italians (that both grew up speaking English in the same town), Toronto is quite diverse, so this type of cross-cultural narrative was accepted at large by the progressive local theater audiences at the turn of the century (i.e., circa way back in 2004).

Our friend Charles Ketchabaw was the show's producer. Charles and I came up with a press kit idea we called "Jimmy and Vito's 2-4-1 Pizza & Press Kit." First, we bought about a dozen plain white, medium-sized cardboard pizza boxes. We created a logo for the pizza press kit boxes with Jimmy & Vito's faces superimposed over their respective countries' flags. Inside the box contained all the things mentioned that should go into a press kit.

Then just to make things difficult, we arranged deliveries of these press kits to all the applicable major media outlets in Toronto. Applicable outlets, meaning we didn't give The Sports Network a pizza to try to interest them in discussing a play that wasn't about sports. The delivery consisted of the press kit box, plus a second box of actual fresh pizza. For the actual pizzas (which were topped with half Italian toppings and half Greek) we used Pizza Pizza (a Canadian pizza chain), since it had the most locations. We did our best to deliver as many pizza press kits as we could between 11:00 a.m. and 1:00 p.m., hoping the intended recipients would be on hand to receive them around lunch time. Organizing that pizza pick-up and delivery schedule was the most work I've ever done sending out a damn press release.

I felt this was a relatively clever idea at the time; my wife insists this was a brilliant idea. The media folks who received the pizzas were quite grateful, as were many of their coworkers. And yes, we ended up receiving a decent amount of prepress for our efforts. But, man: So much work.

Although physical press kits are typically unnecessary in this day and age, they can be used effectively if you really want to go the extra mile. A strong, original press kit can serve as a great introduction, and as a creative extension of you and what you're doing. As in the culinary world, presentation is the first bite.

1. So Why Is a Press Kit Not Necessary?

All of the main components of a press kit can and should be made available online. These are called Electronic Press Kits (EPKs). An EPK is essentially a website that contains the various elements listed above.

Yet, even an EPK isn't necessarily needed should you structure your press release the way Steve suggested in Chapter 4. All of the components of a press kit can be made into embedded links within your press release, making the release itself an EPK of sorts. Short, simple, and concise — just as the media likes it.

CHAPTER EIGHT

SOCIAL MEDIA WHORE: STEVE'S GUIDE TO SOCIAL MEDIA

Hey gang, Steve here again. To throw a little light jargon at you, social media is the blanket term for computer-mediated, virtual communities featuring user-generated content. And it can be your best friend when it comes to promoting your thing. OK, "best friend" may be a bit off the mark. Let's say your friend with benefits. That sounds more accurate. And sexier.

If you're younger than 110, chances are you're on social media in one form or another. And at the risk of quickly making this book seem dated, I'm going to name a few of these outlets. I'm well aware online trends change very quickly, which is why there haven't been any reprints of my 1999 relationship guide, *I See Cupid: How to Find Your Soulmate on ICQ*. Anyhow, current social media juggernauts include Facebook, Twitter, Instagram, YouTube, Tumblr, LinkedIn, and SnapChat. Maybe Pinterest? Sure, why not. Etsy? OK, that's starting to push it.

With traditional media, the coverage your thing receives is a cocreation of you and the media contact who takes an interest in it. By contrast, social media is 200 percent you. (I actually meant to type 100 percent there, but 200 percent came out instead, so whatever, I'm leaving it.) On social media, there's no third party editor or story committee; what you put out there is completely in your hands.

Is social media mandatory when getting your thing out there? Maybe not, but it's very recommended these days. Think of it as a high-quality arrow in your quiver. A powerful 3 wood in your golf bag. A versatile blank tile in your Scrabble game. Believe me, I'm prepared to throw another 20 or 30 dumb analogies your way. Bottom line: Social media is a solid — and mostly free — companion to traditional media when you're trying to spread the word about your thing. Here are a few tips for using it to your advantage:

- At the very least, nab yourself Facebook, Twitter, YouTube, and Instagram accounts. You likely have at least one or two of these already, if not all four. When it comes to your thing, you can use your preexisting accounts, given that you already have some sort of a following on them. Alternately, you can create a new set of accounts dedicated solely to your thing.

- Create a Facebook Event for your thing, and invite everyone you know, encouraging them to do the same. For every person that shares it, your reach continues to expand.

- Create a searchable hashtag for your thing (e.g., #MyAwesomeThing), one you'll use across all your social media platforms. Heck, place it on emails, invites, posters, handouts, even your press releases — pretty much any forms of communication you can. That's called branding, cousin, and it honestly makes a difference. Be sure your hashtag is unique enough: #book or #concert will get your thing lumped in with a whole bunch of crap that isn't yours.

- Social media is a two-way street, so get folks to not simply receive your information, but engage in it. Most platforms now have a polling option, where your audience can take part in a fun survey related to your thing. Do you have the budget for a small contest or giveaway? Make it happen, (e.g., "The person who shares the largest number of my posts this week will win this spectacular prize!").

- A picture is worth a 1,000 words, and let's face it, most folks don't like reading more than a couple hundred words. So whenever possible, consider eye-catching images on your pages. Is your thing a yearly, monthly, or weekly event? If so, post pictures, with catchy, informative captions of its previous iterations. If this is your first go-round, you can post teasers or behind-the-scenes images to pique people's interest. Once your thing has launched, consider uploading highlight pics and video.

- Here's a dumb but memorable Johnny Cochran-style rhyme: Be great, don't inundate. In other words, the quickest way to get blocked or silenced on social media is to post too damn often. So the key is to find the sweet spot, where your thing stays on folks' radars without burning them out.

- Does your thing take place at a specific day and time? If so, encourage, and participate in live tweeting. Naturally, you'll want to see that ubiquitous hashtag of yours on every tweet.

- Host a live video chat session. Whether you use Facebook, SnapChat, Ustream, or another platform, a live chat session (i.e., a Q & A) can encourage investment, involvement, interaction, and incentive.

- Speaking of incentive, consider attaching registration windows and early bird deadlines to your thing via social media posts. Informing friends, family, and strangers about your thing is important, but it's all for naught if they don't pull the trigger and lay down their money. Psychologically, we're all drawn to getting better deals than other people. Which is why an incentivizing "ticking clock" can go a long way.

It's never a bad idea to build up a strong social media presence in general, as this can help you curry favor with the regular media — not just with your current thing, but your future things as well. In 2016, a talented local performer, Megan MacKay, hired us to publicize a new comedy project. And what made our jobs a heck of a lot easier was the fact she already had a very decent social media presence: 6,500 Twitter followers, and nearly 50,000 YouTube subscribers. This popularity played a big role nabbing her TV and radio interviews.

Another example is the time we served as publicists for WWE announcer and hall of famer Jim Ross. Whenever a media contact was on the fence about covering a wrestling personality, we'd simply point out the 1-million-plus Twitter followers who'd be tweeted a link to any interview he'd give. This was almost always enough to turn a maybe into a yes.

So trust me, upping your social media game will never be a waste of time. And as always, if you get befuddled at the slightest thing technical, you've got at least ten friends who are total pros, and they'll be happy to help for free. Or for some beer. Everyone does things for beer.

CHAPTER NINE

SIMPLE MARKETING TIPS FOR PROMOTING YOUR THING LOCALLY

When I was handling publicity for The Second City, people would often say to me, "I saw the Second City poster on the subway! Great job!" I would then explain the posters they saw were set up by the marketing department and "I had nothing to do with that, but thank you anyway!" The marketing department of any company is responsible for coming up with creative ads and promotions. Publicity and marketing, although different jobs, do go hand in hand. Media attention I'd obtain, such as pull-quotes and star ratings, would be used in specific ads created by the marketing department.

Anyone starting out with any sort of creative endeavor (e.g., a person reading this book) is not likely to have his or her own marketing department. When you're an independent producer/ business owner, you are the marketing department. I've been this person many times, so although this book is focused on obtaining media attention, here are some general ground-level marketing ideas to consider for the "budgetarily challenged."

Also: Keep in mind that if you want attention, you have to somehow think of how your thing is newsworthy or attention-worthy, and work that into your materials.

1. Promotional Material (Posters, Flyers, Programs)

An entire book could be written about the dos and don'ts of creating a good poster. If you have no idea what makes a good poster, allow me to say this: You do know. You've seen many posters/flyers in your life, and you're well aware of what works. A great poster is subjective, of course, but a bad poster should be pretty obvious.

Let's assume you already have a poster for your thing. Perhaps you designed it yourself, or you had someone do it for you and you're happy with it. Now what?

If you intend to design, print, and distribute posters in a traditional fashion, this process can end up being expensive. When you're first starting out, more often than not everything is paid for from your personal budget. The assumption is that you don't personally own an industrial photocopier that can print out a mass set of glossy color posters. You may be in a situation where you must rely upon paying for this service with a public copy place. Then again, maybe you don't.

Perhaps you don't own a photocopier; however, you work for a company that does. The next logical and obvious step is to steal as many copies as you possibly can when nobody's looking. Cover your tracks and don't leave the original in the machine. Then clear the job history from the computer, wipe your prints from the machine, and erase the security tapes. Easy.

Or you may be one of these people who thinks you are better than me and doesn't wish to steal from your employer. Well then, I suppose it doesn't hurt to ask. Ask your employer if you can set up an arrangement to use the photocopier so you can potentially save yourself a lot of money. What kind of arrangement? A sponsorship arrangement. You can ask if he or she is willing to be a sponsor for your thing in exchange for the use of the copier. In turn, you can offer to add your company's logo to all of your promotional material. If this idea doesn't resonate with the employer, it can still work elsewhere. Many places obviously have photocopiers, which means there are many places to which you can reach out for such an arrangement. Remember, it's always quicker to make arrangements with independent establishments than a company with a head office in another city.

Putting up posters yourself around your city/town can be very time consuming and frustrating. Frustrating because, depending on where you live, you're under the rule of local postering laws. In others words, you can spend eight hours putting up outdoor posters around town, only for them to be taken down the next day by a city worker. Or worse, postered over by the Poster Mafia (more on these saints shortly). Again this all depends on local ordinances, so be aware of them before going through all that effort. If you're eager enough, and feel confident your postering efforts won't be in vain, then grab yourself a bucket, some liquid adhesive, a cart full of posters, and hit the streets! I did this countless times back in the day. Although admittedly I have no real desire to ever do it again.

When I chose to indulge in this not-particularly-glamorous task, I found the most effective approach involved indoor postering. I'm referring to the insides of independent establishments: restaurants, cafés, bookstores, gyms, flower shops, dry cleaners, etc. Many of these places are very kind and in tune with their community. Which means they often have a place on one of their walls earmarked for local event posters. Simply step inside, say hello to the person in charge, and ask if you could please put up a poster. Chances are, it won't be taken down by anyone until your event is over, nor will it be subjected to weather damage. Sure, the process is still very time consuming, but you'll be far happier with the results.

1.1 Beware of the Poster Mafia

In our society, for every job you don't want to do there's someone willing to do it for money. There are companies in most mid- to large-sized cities you can hire to put up your posters, both indoors and out. When I've been blessed with a budget, I've hired a few of them. And rarely was I satisfied with the results. Why?

In many cities, they're constantly engaged in a turf war with one another.

After the events of September 11, 2001, the Toronto comedy community held a benefit at The Second City for those affected. Several of us put in our own money for promotion, and paid for a postering service to plaster our event throughout the downtown core. A day after we used this service, I received a phone call. It came from someone who didn't give me his name but made sure to tell me which postering service he worked for. He called to inform me he just spent the last several hours postering over our posters, and that he would continue to do so if we didn't immediately hire his company. I said to him, "You do realize this is a charity event you're postering over?" His response: "You have until 6:00 p.m. or the rest of them are gone."

I'm not going to mention this classy organization by name, as I don't wish to get whacked in the back of the head in a drive-by, by some cyclist dude with a wet squeegee. The moral here is to do it yourself. Or, at the very least, find out who the most dominant Poster Mafia is in your area.

2. Sponsorship

If your event warrants a program or any form of printed take-away element, you have an opportunity to attract local sponsorship. Some such events include theater productions, art exhibits, or small festivals of any kind. If you're creating programs or flyers, you're automatically generating advertising space. The printing costs can be offset the same way as your posters. Simply approach businesses in the vicinity of the venue. As with the media, email is the best way to initiate first contact.

Alternately, you can create physical packages containing a sponsorship letter request, along with information about the event. It's easy enough to drop these off in person — not only will you save money, but a face-to-face encounter can go a long way. Simply explain who you are, what you're producing, and ask if they'd consider purchasing reasonably priced advertising space in your programs, posters, or both. Don't come to them expecting an answer on the spot. Just explain what you are doing and leave them the package for consideration. Come armed with information, such as the capacity of the venue and, an estimate of how many people would receive a program (or flyer) throughout the run. If you're offering to have their logo appear on your poster, confirm how many posters would be distributed around town.

When you're working independently, every dollar counts. So it's in your best interest to be reasonable when asking for help. I was always grateful for any sponsorship money obtained, and would happily take $50 or $100 for a half page ad if that was the offer on the table, or more for a full back page ad. If you're fortunate enough to obtain multiple sponsors, it's not difficult to add extra space to all of your promotional material.

2.1 Media sponsors

Your local media is often quite involved with events around town. Which makes them very open to becoming media sponsors. And just as with nabbing media attention, media sponsorship can be obtained by simply asking for it. Charity events often have an advantage here, but not exclusively.

So what does media sponsorship usually entail? Here's an example: If a local newspaper becomes your media sponsor, it will typically place ads in its paper (and on its website) for your upcoming event. At no cost, naturally. In turn you're expected to place the media sponsor's ad or logo on all promotional material. (The volume and the size of the advertising will vary depending on the agreement you make.) This can be highly beneficial if the newspaper reflects the demographic you're aiming to reach. That said, when this newspaper becomes your sponsor, exclusivity is generally expected. This means you can't always make similar deals with rival media outlets. As well, be aware this newspaper may be owned by a parent company, one that also owns several radio and TV stations. Meaning you may not be able to approach media outlets across several platforms once the ink has dried on your sponsorship contract. Still, the pros here can often out-weigh the cons.

Media companies are approached for sponsorship all the time. On the occasions I've asked for this privilege, I first reached out via email to set up an in-person meeting with a representative in their advertising department. Come prepared to this meeting with as much information you have, as well as a few good reasons why this particular media outlet is a good fit for your event.

2.2 Business Improvement Areas (BIAs) and local government sponsorship

In 1970 Toronto, as the dirty socialists we were, we formed the world's first Business Improvement Area (BIA) group. A BIA is a collection of local businesses that meet up on a regular basis (usually monthly) to discuss ways to improve various initiatives, as well as the community as a whole. Since then, this model has been replicated all over the world. Hopefully there's a similar business collective where you live. If not, consider approaching your local government about forming one.

If you've never attended a BIA meeting, I suggest doing so, since they can be pretty fascinating. Aside from local businesses owners, expect to find anyone from police officers to municipal government officials in attendance. Over the years, I've attended several meetings in different BIAs for the purpose of obtaining assistance with promoting an event. I would first contact the BIA in the area where I was staging a production. I'd then ask to attend the next scheduled meeting and explain what I wished to discuss. If the BIA had time for me (and it usually did), I would come equipped with my trusty sponsorship information.

With the interest of the BIA in mind, I'd explain why my event would bring scores of new people into its neighborhood. The kind of people who'd have an interest in local bars, restaurants, and shops associated with the BIA. The group would then vote on my proposal right then and there, determining whether or not to allocate funds for the event. Sometimes I'd request a specific dollar amount; other times I'd simply shut up and let the group offer me something. The most I ever received from a BIA was $500, which is an amazing amount of money for attending a meeting. Thank you to all the BIAs!

CHAPTER TEN

FRIENDS WITH BENEFITS: DOING MEDIA FOR OTHERS BENEFITS YOU

When I started doing this type of work, Steve and I did many free jobs for our creative friends. Not because people didn't offer to pay — or that we were particularly nice people — but because at first we didn't feel right charging for a service we were still figuring out as we went along.

As stated before, nothing you do will ever be in vain when applying this information. Over time, the benefits of these jobs became clear. We'd offer our services to the people we sincerely respected and admired as artists. This would allow for us to attach our names to interesting projects. This in turn would allow for us to get better results, as it's much easier to convey real excitement about something you genuinely like and respect. Even though we were contacting the media regarding other people's projects, it was still *us* making contact. And this allowed us to develop and maintain a working relationship — and sometimes even friendship — with people in the media.

When you work with highly creative individuals who are also consistent, it's only a matter of time before they excel. Over time, many of the people we assisted with our publicity services have grown into various positions of power within their respected industries. The majority of our higher-profile media jobs can be linked back to a gig we had once done for free.

Providing publicity services for others isn't only good practice for your own endeavors, it can also just feel good. It's enjoyable to help shine the light on someone you feel deserves it. And there's nothing like the feeling of telling a friend the media will be writing an article about his or her passion project. Personally, I love when people tell me their mom called all of her friends to watch them on TV.

1. Assisting with Local Charities

It feels good to shine a light on a charity you believe in. If there's a grassroots organization you support, why not offer to assist with its media outreach, should you feel so inclined. It's excellent practice for you, and the organization you're assisting will be eternally grateful.

You can also incorporate a charity into your own project in a seamless, mutually beneficial way. For example, your sketch comedy troupe is putting on a show. The troupe's new to the scene and therefore relatively unknown to the local media. You decide some — or all — of the show's proceeds will go to your charity of choice. By teaming up with an established local charity, it, in turn, becomes part of your attraction, thereby raising everyone's profile. Once again, win-win.

We suggest grassroots organizations for a few reasons. First, you're more likely to speak with the individual in charge to create an arrangement. And more often than not, they'll greatly appreciate your desire to help. This isn't to say larger nonprofits like the Red Cross won't appreciate your efforts. But smaller organizations are typically in a better position to help you in return. They often have extensive mailing lists, and can easily spread the word about your upcoming event.

2. Philanthropic Marketing

Philanthropy is the future of marketing.

— STEPHANIE MCMAHON, CHIEF BRAND OFFICER FOR WWE

When I first heard this quote, it felt somewhat dirty and I didn't like it. It seemed to encapsulate the negative connotation one might apply to the term "media whore," suggesting charitable donations are there to make you look good in the media. If I choose to frame this idea as such, it certainly sounds negative. Stephanie McMahon received a ton of online backlash for this statement. As a fan of both Stephanie McMahon and the WWE, I can't really speak for what she truly meant. And despite how I may have felt when initially reading this quote, objectively I can't deny there's something to it.

Let's elaborate. The WWE is a company that does a lot of charity work, and it's not shy about letting you know about it. The WWE, bless them, are total media whores. John Cena, a center-piece of this company, is not someone I would consider a media whore. As of the publishing date of this book, the wrestler/actor has granted more than 500 wishes for the Make-A-Wish foundation. Imagine: 500! On 500 occasions, this man dropped every-thing in his already busy life to make time for ailing children. This is far more than any other celebrity in the history of the Make-A-Wish organization. Cena doesn't tout this fact himself, but the WWE certainly does, and why not? It's a very beautiful thing this man continues to do.

If you're a fan of improv comedy, you're likely aware who Colin Mochrie is. Worldwide, he's best known for his excellent comedic work on the hit TV show *Whose Line Is It Anyway?* Lucky for me, Colin lives in my city. Luckier for me, as well as for many others, Colin is one of the nicest and most charitable people with whom I've ever had the pleasure of meeting and working. If there's a charity benefit and Colin is in town, you can bet he'll be there.

How has Colin Mochrie benefited me, as well as others? There are honestly countless examples. One dates back to 2004, when a devastating tsunami struck Indonesia. Steve and I, as well as several of our friends from the Toronto comedy community, got together to put on a benefit for those affected by the disaster. From my perspective as a producer/promoter, I always wanted to put on the best show possible, regardless of the reason it was taking place. This particular benefit was staged at The Second City, which held 400 people. At the time I was more accustomed to staging shows in the building's secondary theater, which held 120. Producing this benefit allowed for me to reach out to Colin, as well as other notable performers. Having Colin join allowed me to secure the main theater for this event, as Second City bosses saw it as a bigger deal. Colin was extremely generous with his time, agreeing to do every media interview I could get for him. This wasn't a difficult sell to the media, as you can imagine, and his presence allowed for the event to sell out and raise a lot of money. Extra credit to The Second City, which agreed to match the dollar amount we raised. To boot, the Canadian government then stepped in and matched the total dollar amount raised, which came to approximately $24,000. Not bad, eh?

To summarize this point: The charity led to the celebrity. The charity and the celebrity led to the desired venue. These combined elements led me to pitching the media about something they were very interested in. The sum of all these efforts led to a lot of money going to the charity.

What did I get out of this? A great show, with great people, in a great venue, that allowed me to obtain great media coverage for the charity and everyone involved. What more could I have asked for?

When I choose to give this meaning to the idea of philanthropic marketing, it doesn't sound so bad, does it?

CHAPTER ELEVEN

REVIEWS:
HOW TO WELCOME SOLICITED
JUDGMENT INTO YOUR LIFE

If you have no critics you'll likely have no success.

— MALCOLM X

You breathe life into an idea you love and develop it into a thing. You give it all your free time and focus. So much so that you may even refer to this thing as your baby.

Then this strange need comes along to invite a person you don't know to judge your baby thing. Specifically, to share this judgment with a larger group of people you also don't know. This sounds like an awful idea.

Sweet, crazy, lovely friends, we're not here to judge your egos for wanting validation from the masses (just as we wouldn't judge you for giving this book a five-star review). Whether you give this book five stars out of five, or six stars out of five, it doesn't matter. None of this matters. Reviews are meaningless aside from the meaning you give them.

Here's a short, completely objective review of this chapter so far:

The quote "Reviews are meaningless aside from the meaning you give them" came off as quite profound and meaningful.

— Daniel Shehori

You may feel that writing a review for yourself is pointless; therefore, in itself meaningless. You may question the proclaimed objectivity of this review. What does this mean when you feel your opinions about yourself to be meaningless, yet the opinions of strangers can affect your day?

The chapter continued to ask deep philosophical questions while simultaneously bringing forth insights that allowed the reader to truly resonate with the answers.

— Daniel Shehori

Meaningless sentiments and rhetorical questions aside, let's discuss getting reviewed! There are certainly many advantages to having your thing professionally assessed. Especially if it's good. A strong point to reiterate here is that reviews (and media in general) should not be solely relied on for attracting people to your thing. Consider reviews an enhancement at best.

If you're Guns N' Roses, rolling through town for one night only, the show is likely to be reviewed by the major media outlets in the region. If you're just starting out, it's more likely you'll be reviewed based on the number of opportunities people have to see it. For example, if you're staging a play or a music show for one night only, the chances of being reviewed decrease, as you're giving people a small window of time to come see it. A newspaper writer has little incentive to write about something readers can't see for themselves by the time the review comes out. To be clear, you can certainly try to obtain prepress for a one-night event, however, it is far tougher to obtain reviews.

Reviews may not be important to you at all. They can either be ignored, or they can be utilized in multiple ways, such as attracting representation, jobs within your specific field, corporate sponsorship, government grants, and work visas. A good review in Toronto will help when you're trying to obtain prepress in Vancouver, New York, or Chicago.

1. So I'm Just Going to Ask for People in the Media to Come Review My Thing, Right?

Correct. Same as before. The more notice the better. If you're promoting something time sensitive such as a theater production, inviting reviewers can be done in varying degrees of formal. In case you're unaware, it's customary that members of the media receive two complimentary tickets to your event. At first, it's best you arrange a reviewer by contacting the editor of the newspaper. Trying to arrange for a review is a solid, organic reason to follow up with someone after the press release has gone out. If you've established a relationship with a reviewer over time, you can contact this person directly. There is a new generation of independent reviewers that write for all sorts of online publications. Be sure to seek them out if reviews are important to you.

1.1 Negative reviews

Everyone you've admired that has been reviewed about anything has received a negative blurb at some point. Steve and I certainly have. We once wrote and directed a comedic play and entered it into the Toronto Fringe Festival. (We keep bringing up this festival.) The Toronto Fringe is an annual summer theater festival that consists of approximately 120 independent shows. There are similar types of festivals all over the world. We were allotted eight time slots over eleven days. We worked very hard on this production; entering a play you're proud of in a large festival is a full-time job in the months leading up to it. We cast the production with the very best people we were fortunate enough to convince to work with us. We're blessed with talented friends so we really did have top-notch comedic actors at our disposal.

We worked countless hours on the script, trying to make it funny and original. We, of course, took on the task of trying to obtain media attention, competing against 120 other shows. We did relatively well, considering.

And then, as you may have suspected from the title of this section, we received a very disparaging review. This review came from the beloved *NOW Magazine*, a weekly Toronto arts/culture publication. The magazine that if you're an aspiring artist in Toronto, you want shining its light on you. Instead of a star system, *NOW* uses the "N" system for rating purposes. Our rating: NN (out of five.) If only that was the worst of it. That week NOW dedicated an entire page to what they didn't like at the Fringe. And under the headline "Lame Laughs" was a large color photo of Steve and me. Despite our show getting the best review in the article, we became the poster boys for all that was bad at that year's festival.

We didn't enjoy this feeling, to say the least. We were angry and confused and it drained a lot of positive energy from us going forward. Especially since we still had four shows left to perform. Although I didn't agree with what was written about us at the time, I'm grateful for still having the sense to not lash out at *NOW Magazine*. Specifically, at the writer of the review: Glenn Sumi. It was tempting.

1.2 The positive from all this negative

There has been an abundance of good that has come from this situation. Perhaps most valuable is the greater perspective we gained as to what we were doing. We came to realize that although we took it quite personally at the time it certainly wasn't personal with Glenn Sumi. We realized that many of our favorite artists have also received negative reviews from Glenn Sumi. Eventually the negative review felt like a rite of passage. I like Glenn Sumi the human being a lot and very much respect the time and effort he puts into his work. Since then Sumi has granted us and the clients we work for more media attention than I can honestly remember; more than 50 articles and reviews since he slapped us with that NN. The NN wasn't personal. He just didn't care for what we were doing at that time relative to all the other shows he watched that week during the festival. I'd gladly exchange one bad review for thousands upon thousands of dollars worth of media obtained since. Even though I was horrified about the "Lame Laughs" article at the time I wish I could show it to you now for this book. However I can't, because Glenn Sumi did a really nice thing for us after the fact by having it wiped from the Internet. (I didn't go out of my way to save a hard copy of this article either.) Glenn certainly didn't have to do that. Thank you, Glenn.

Also worth noting about that Fringe Festival experience: We received very positive reviews from other media outlets, and our entire run was sold out. So thankfully, the bad review didn't affect people's interest in the production. Although in hindsight, it doesn't rank particularly high on my personal list of shows we've created. Nowadays, I'd even consider it kind of lame by comparison.

In an attempt to find the positive in a negative review, people sometimes resort to cherry picking words out of context. I don't encourage this type of action; you'll get caught, and it's not worth the further negative backlash you will receive for doing so.

For example, the 2015 film *Accidental Love* (or *Nailed* as it was called in Canada for some reason) was called a "comedic masterstroke" by The Onion's *The A.V. Club*. Except for the small fact it didn't call it that at all. The company in charge of marketing and distributing the film called it that. *The A.V. Club* reviewer, A.A. Dowd, actually wrote: "To be fair to whoever refashioned *Accidental Love* from the abandoned scraps of *Nailed*, there's little reason to believe that the ideal, untroubled version of the material would have been a comedic masterstroke."

Again, I understand why people go to such lengths, but I strongly discourage behavior such as twisting the words of reviewers. To his credit, Mr. Dowd didn't allow these folks to get away with their publicity con; he penned a very funny and poignant open letter titled, "No, I didn't call your shitty movie a 'comedic masterstroke.'"

There is no form of art so good that it's immune to negative criticism. Just hit YouTube and see how many goofs have clicked "thumbs down" to Beethoven's Ninth Symphony. How you choose to respond to reviews, good or bad, is completely up to you. People will have no problem sharing links to positive reviews throughout all forms of social media. You should too. Just don't be too much of a whore about it. More on this later.

CHAPTER TWELVE

MORE ON WHY IT NEVER HURTS TO ASK (OR: CAREFUL WHAT YOU ASK FOR, OR YOU MIGHT JUST GET THE FRONT PAGE OF THE *TORONTO SUN*. TWICE.)

If you're not careful, the newspapers will have you hat-ing the people who are being oppressed, and loving the people who are doing the oppressing.

— MALCOLM X

Two Malcolm X quotes in two consecutive chapters? Damn, this book got serious.

1. Careful What You Wish For

In early 2010, Steve and I were sharing the information from this book in a class we taught through Toronto's Second City Training Centre. At one point, we conducted an exercise where attendees would come up with press release angles for an upcoming proj-ect of theirs. Catherine Frid raised her hand, volunteering to kick things off. Catherine had written a play called *Homegrown*, which was selected to be staged at the SummerWorks theater festival that August.

Homegrown is a play about Shareef Abdelhaleem, a man charged with, and later convicted of, homegrown terrorism for conspiring to set off a bomb in downtown Toronto. Catherine is a law school graduate who studied this case at great length (enough that she felt confident to write a play about it). When she shared the play's details with the class, Steve and I assured her that she had enough angles to fill several press releases. As publicists, you never want to guarantee results, since our friends in the media can be unpredictable. However, we broke our own rule in this instance, guaranteeing Catherine she'd get a strong response from a well-written press release.

Catherine followed up on the notes she took in class, wrote a terrific press release, and set out to engage the Toronto media. Engage them she certainly did. The response was far greater than Catherine or Steve and I could have imagined. At first the *Toronto Star* responded. Not the Arts section but a section called Greater Toronto. The *Star* writer asked to see a rehearsal of *Homegrown*. End result: Catherine's play nabbed a cover story of the GT section. Amazing!

However, this was just the start. Soon after, every major Canadian media outlet wanted a piece of this story. On July 31, 2010, Catherine's play made the cover of *Toronto Sun*, one of the country's largest newspapers. As in the front cover.

The cover consisted of a photo of her lead actor with the headline "Sympathy for the DEVIL." The subtitle read, "Your tax dollars help stage a play that portrays terrorist in positive light." Worth noting that the production had yet to be released, and nobody from the *Sun* had viewed the rehearsal, or even a script. A week later, the *Toronto Sun* — still not satisfied — graciously gave Catherine's play another front cover. This time with a photo of a daughter of a 9/11 victim holding the *Homegrown* program with the headline "Play hits home." I suppose this type of attention from the *Sun* contradicts what we said about all prepress being positive. That said, *Homegrown* was very popular at the festival, so clearly the financial impact was positive.

As mentioned, Catherine's play received attention from much of the major media in Canada. Some co-opting a similar tone as the *Sun*, and others just wanting to discuss the merits of the from a theatrical standpoint. The Prime Minister of Canada at the time,

Stephen Harper, even spoke about the production, saying he was "concerned." Was he concerned for Catherine's well-being, given she was now receiving threats online? Seemingly no. A spokesperson for the Prime Minister said Harper was "extremely disappointed that public money is being used to fund plays that glorify terrorism."

The following year, SummerWorks lost its federal arts funding. This is what you get for raising your hand in class.

Fortunately, none of this has deterred Catherine; she very much remains persistent and consistent, constantly creating new work and engaging the media as she goes along.

Side note: In 2012, Steve and I wrote and directed a satirical musical produced by The Second City called *Stephen Harper: The Musical!* It toured across Canada, and not a damn peep did we hear from the Prime Minister about this.

On a lighter note, in the summer of 2011, Steve and I were approached by the Toronto-based charity Lake Ontario Waterkeepers. Our friend Jackie Mersereau was working with the organization at the time, and asked if we could assist with a media job. The Waterkeepers were about to launch an app that informed people which beaches in their area were open and safe for swimming. I knew very little about the Waterkeepers, and at the time I didn't even own a smartphone to check out the app. Not surprisingly, I wasn't entirely sure how to present this story to the media, or how it would even play out. All I was going on was that the app sounded cool, the charity had nice people, and Jackie was a good friend. As such, I was armed with little more than my desire to make this work out.

I reached out to a writer at the *National Post* named Ben Kaplan. I had worked with Ben in the past on other stories, and I knew he had an open mind to such things. So I thought to myself, "It never hurts to ask." Specifically, I figured it wouldn't hurt to explain to Ben what the app did, and see if *The National Post* might have some space for a tiny bit of coverage.

Ben in turn loved the story and the app. So much so that he turned it into a cover story, which included a two-page color spread for the paper's Toronto section. I didn't expect a cover story from this, and I certainly didn't ask for it. Not that I didn't feel it was worthy, but the idea that a politically conservative national newspaper would run a cover story about an environmental app; it was the longest of longshots. To Ben, however, this was just the kind of thing he was looking for. Sometimes you just never know. Thank you, Ben.

2. GASH – North America's Only Band

Back in 2000, when we were first starting out with all this media stuff, one of my best friends, Mark McIntyre, had a dream. Mark is an actor who also wanted to be a rock star. I offered him a slot on a comedy variety show I was producing at my favorite venue, The Tim Sims Playhouse. The Playhouse closed down a couple of years later, making way for the Diesel Playhouse, which has also since closed down. This venue was also many things before this, including a nightclub, a sports bar, maybe an orphanage or something, and originally a house that burnt down twice. It's now a condo/hotel. You know, for now. Anyway, Mark performed a song on my variety show. One detailing a true-life experience where after getting drunk at a wedding, he wet the bed he was sharing with one of the bridesmaids. Mark somewhere found a ridiculous, long blond rocker wig and decided to try his best to talk like Paul Stanley from KISS. Backstage prior to the show, Mark asked me what I thought about the name "Gash" for his character. "I don't see why not," I believe is what I told him. After performing this heartfelt song (titled "Michelle") — a ballad about inadvertently urinating on another human being — it was clear Mark had an idea that could grow into something more substantial.

Note: When I refer to "Gash," I mean the person (Mark). When I refer to "GASH" I mean the entire band. Thought you should know.

Anyhow, things moved quickly from this point on, and before we knew it, GASH turned into a four-person comedy glam rock ensemble that both satirized and embraced 1980s heavy metal culture. Objectively, as always, I adored this band. Gash himself was very funny, however I also really loved the music. Gash may have started as a fictional comedy character, but the boys in the band made it quite real. I loved the crowds it would attract, as well as the theatrics of the performances. We even sold merch. I loved GASH so much that I took it upon myself to manage the band, which involved booking gigs and — of course — generating media attention. My other duty as manager was to pull up Gash's pants during the performance when called for. This happened once a show (a long story involving Bob Marley encouraging Gash to consider the idea of wearing speedos). Steve was also in GASH for a while as the original bass player, Bitchin' Mitchell Rhodes. He even came up with the tagline for the T-shirts: GASH — North America's only band. (Not including Mexico.)

Prior to the existence of GASH, we had mostly been doing publicity work for theater and comedy events. I had yet to engage anyone from the music media. Which meant I was starting from zero with a strange novelty act. The music scene in Toronto is, in my perception, ten times the size of the comedy scene, with countless local acts of myriad genres performing nightly across the city. This challenge helped us learn that it didn't matter what we were trying to promote. As long as we kept applying the publicity ideas we'd developed, the results would appear. And yep, the results eventually did appear. GASH kept being consistent, and I kept being persistent.

While Mark borrowed from Paul Stanley, I borrowed a marketing tactic from its KISS cofounder, Gene Simmons. When trying to book shows and attract media attention for GASH simultaneously, one strategy I'd often pull was as follows: I'd reach out to more established bands with a compatible sound to GASH. To me, an established band meant they were consistently drawing 200+ people to their events. I'd offer to set up a show where they headline at a venue they'd enjoy in exchange for allowing GASH to open for them. All they had to do was show up and we'd handle everything. Including media attention. I'd then reach out to a fresh new band that's still likely to bring out all of their friends. The hope was a band like this would attract anywhere between 25 to 50 people. Sometimes more. This band would go on first, followed by GASH and then the headliner. The goal was to maximize the amount of people that would watch GASH by simply drawing from the other bands' fans.

When executed successfully, the venues' owners would be happy, since their establishments would be crammed with people buying drinks. This approach allowed me to book more GASH shows in the future. The headliner was happy, as GASH fans would usually stay to watch them, and the opening band was happy to be on a show with a notable headliner. Meanwhile, I was happy, because I could utilize these more established acts as a selling point when I spoke to the music media about GASH.

There was never a shortage of bands from out of town I could contact. I'd look at the upcoming events calendar at the venues I wanted GASH to book, and would reach out to the bands that had booked so far ahead, they had yet to consider an opening act. This worked best with indie bands, as bands signed to labels don't often make these decisions themselves. Often the label will just stick another act from their roster on the lineup. Although not every band and venue had an interest in my offer, some did, and that made all the difference.

Unlike our negative experience at the Fringe with *NOW Magazine*, GASH received a NNNN review for one of its live shows and an NNNN review for its debut EP. These proved to be helpful moving forward. Once, with a well-made press kit consisting of the album and these glowing reviews, GASH was invited to headline a music festival in Halifax. An impressive development, given we merely asked politely if GASH could attend. Sadly, this festival was cancelled before GASH got there, but this is hardly the point. GASH wasn't headed to the east coast to merely headline one measly festival. The band made a stop along the way in Charlottetown, PE, to perform at the local rock venue Melons. A band like GASH was meant to play in a venue called Melons. We obtained an entertainment section cover story from the *Charlottetown*

Guardian. (Once again, we never asked to be on the front page, just for a bit of coverage.)

Legend has it, as I wasn't in the room for this, a team of music execs at SONY once sat around a table and listened to GASH. I was told they loved it but didn't know what they would do with it, so they eventually passed. Still, a victory. Hey, this went from a joke character at a local comedy show to getting a CD into the hands of SONY. Mark believed in himself and in his thing (a.k.a., his band), and when you put yourself out there like he did, you never know where it can lead. GASH was an extremely fun ride that was also a tremendous learning experience for all involved.

So what happened to GASH? Did the band give up after this blow from SONY? No, not really but the guitar player (Deuce Diamond) and his wife had twin boys. The Diamond family then moved to Halifax from Toronto to raise the family, hence ending the consistency of the band. No regrets. Deuce's wife, soon after setting up their new life in Halifax, left him for another woman. Hey, that's rock n' roll — the boys all knew what a crazy world they were getting into. Well, maybe Deuce didn't. Thank you, Deuce.

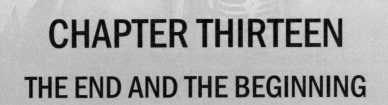

CHAPTER THIRTEEN

THE END AND THE BEGINNING

Steve and I have vastly different mindsets in regards to media as a whole. This may sound odd coming from the author of this material, however I stopped paying attention to the media a long time ago. I stopped reading newspapers, watching television news, and listening to news radio. I don't even seek out news online. To clarify, I do seek out news; however, being rather selfish, I only gravitate toward the information that interests me.

I stopped paying attention on November 5, 2008, to be exact. The day after President Obama was elected. This wasn't out of any sort of protest; I was quite happy he won. I intended on stopping a year earlier; however, up until this point in history, rap music kept telling me there would never be a black president, so I wanted to see this storyline through to the end.

Steve, on the other hand, is very much on top of current events and takes an active creative role in the media by writing for several magazines. These include the *Huffington Post*, *The A/V Club*, and *Splitsider*. He also writes for television and hosts a weekly podcast (whose press release you deconstructed in Chapter 4). Heck, sometimes I even get to have Steve write articles on the media projects we're working on.

Hey, isn't that a conflict of interest? Probably, but there's no conflict in my interests.

The point is, the information in this book can be useful to you regardless of your current knowledge of the media. *Media Whore* has been designed so that it doesn't matter if you start at the last chapter and read back to Chapter 1. You'll learn the key points easily, regardless of how you come at it. Some of you may have also noticed this book is written in iambic pentameter. I was personally opposed to this literary style, as it felt it a little too flashy. However, I wasn't in the state of mind to argue with the Grand Creator who controlled my fingers and the keyboard utilized to transcribe all this from the Universe. It is what it is.

OK, this isn't written in iambic pentameter. I made that part up. That would have been ridiculously difficult and unnecessary. The part about being able to read this back to front and it still making sense may also be false. I haven't actually tried, as I don't really like reading books. However, I'm told that, if read at the correct pace, *Media Whore* does in fact sync up perfectly with Pink Floyd's *The Dark Side of the Moon*.

1. The Monetary Value of Your Results

One way you can gauge the success of your publicity is to figure out an actual dollar value for your potential results by cross referencing what media outlets charge for advertising. You can do this by going to the websites of a specific outlet and check out their advertising rates page. This information is commonly located under "Advertise with us" or something to this effect. By doing so, you can see firsthand what newspapers charge for space on the printed page (full, half, quarter, as well as other details such as black and white or color.) You can find out what a radio station charges for a 30-second spot. Major radio stations across North America will sell 30-second ad spots ranging from hundreds to thousands of dollars. With television, these numbers may be tripled or more. (And this doesn't include the cost of producing these commercials.) It's very rare that we've booked a radio or television interview that wasn't at least four minutes long. Convert that time into ad rates, and you're looking at a colossal value. To boot, readers, listeners, and viewers are several times more likely to pay attention to these features than the advertising that accompanies them.

Remember: There's zero cost to booking an interview or article, other than your time and willingness.

2. Check Your Local Listings

One thing sometimes overlooked when it comes to local media is the listings section, a.k.a., the portion of a newspaper that lists events taking place at local venues. Print media was the first to offer this free service; however, in recent years it's expanded to local 24-hour TV channels and radio stations. Typically, there's a section on their corresponding websites where you can easily submit a listing for your local event.

The listing will simply entail:

- Name of event

- Name of venue

- Date of event

- Time of event

- Sometimes they will allow room for a website/URL.

Listings are sometimes overlooked in the overall process because if you live somewhere long enough, you may not be checking your local listings when seeking things to do. As a result, this option may not come to mind when you're ready to spread the word about your thing. After all, these are just a few words buried among many other listings. How effective can it be? Often, very.

Consider This Idea: If you live in a place visited by a steady stream of tourists, you'll want to stay on top of the listings in your area. Many curious tourists are looking to experience the nontraditional tourist attractions. If they do nothing more than a search on their phones for local comedy, what they will find is the sum collection of locally available listings. So even if you don't have an article written about your thing that week, it will still appear on many people's radar. It's a free service, so why not take advantage of it?

Let's recap the entire process of being a media whore again, now that you understand it. And if any of this information feels too easy to be true, then good. That's the intent. This entire book can easily be summarized and understood in a few sentences in any language.

MEDIA WHORE the summary, in a few sentences:

If you value your thing, you should let people know about it. And as the thing's creator, you're the best person to speak about it. To boot, you can easily find the media folks best suited to cover it. Do as Steve suggests when writing your press release. Over time you'll find your own way of structuring and wording this information, making it your own. You'll clearly and respectfully ask for media attention. If you don't hear back from the media, this doesn't mean you've done anything wrong. Be patient. You'll be persistent and consistent and, therefore, this will pay off for you. Repeat this process every time you work on something new.

I will put forth a few examples of this summary in different languages. Although note that all of these languages will be written in English. (Globally agreed on as the greatest language of all time.)

MEDIA WHORE for the human language of TYPE A Personalities:

Your thing is really f'n great and everyone should obviously know about it. You, of course, are the best person on this planet to talk about you and your thing. Hunt down the people in the media that are most likely to cover your genius. Do as Steve suggests when writing your press release. Improve upon it if you feel you must. If you don't know how to perform any of the technical aspects, then guilt one of your intelligent friends to do it for you. Ask with calm assertiveness for the media attention you want. If you don't hear back from the media, shut up. Repeat this process every time you do something awesome, you amazing-go-getting-m'f'r!

MEDIA WHORE for the human language of the Spiritually Minded:

Your thing is a loving, creative extension of you, and you're a creative extension of the loving source-energy of the universe. Therefore, you're at one with this source. The people in the media are also at one with the same source-energy, making them easy for you to seek out. Do as Steve suggests when writing your press release. The people needed to assist you along this journey will appear as you move forward along your path. If you don't hear back from the media, you'll make peace with this. Repeat this process with each new creation you manifest, beloveds.

MEDIA WHORE for the human language of the Millennials:

Your thing is literally the best thing ever! Even though all your friends already know about it, courtesy of social media, why not impress your parents by engaging the *archaic* media?

Although you're already entitled to media attention, please be on your best behavior when you ask for it. You know how to do this. Do as Steve suggests when writing your press release. You already know all the technical stuff required, so the rest will be super easy! If you don't hear back from the media, be patient. I said be patient! Yes, you do know how to be patient, stop that! Repeat this process if you feel like it.

3. And in Conclusion

I still don't know how real publicists go about doing this. *Media Whore* merely explains how we go about it. When I was a little kid not once did I utter, "When I grow up I'm going to be a publicist!" I didn't know what that was. If I did, I probably wouldn't have cared at the time. However, since these experiences were all given to me, and reluctantly accepted, I'm now very grateful for this gift. As said in the beginning of the book, Steve and I first started to do this for the primary intent of getting attention for our creative endeavors. The information in this book has indeed helped with our creative careers and has led to fun experiences I never would have imagined.

Our involvement with both publicity and comedy has allowed me to work on events that many fans of comedy only dream of. Back in 2009 we had the pleasure of handling the media for the great Louis C.K. for a two-night engagement in Toronto at the now defunct Diesel Playhouse. Louis C.K., even back then, didn't require a publicist to obtain media attention. He could have sold out these shows with one tweet. So this is not so impressive from that standpoint, given any monkey could have landed him a ton of publicity. However it was these monkeys that got the call to do the job. A good friend of mine, Jake Labow, was the producer of the show (a friend I once did free work for) and asked if I'd help out. I don't bring this up to name drop. Truth be told, I never even got to meet Louis. And he likely has no idea I even worked on his show. All media requests I obtained first went through Jake, who then passed them onto Louis' manager. I never even spoke with Louis directly. I greatly respect Louis C.K., so I see this as a way to say thank you. It's a lovely life bonus to get paid while expressing gratitude. Also, thank you, Jake.

Steve and I were the official publicists for the legendary Second City comedy theater in Toronto for seven years. Again, when you have such talent and history to work with, this job is not difficult. The Second City job was fun, and often came with additional amazing perks. During our tenure as publicists, a very significant event took place. Members of the original *SCTV* cast returned to their stage roots and performed two nights live in our intimate 300-seat theater for a charity event. If you're not familiar with *SCTV*, the cast that performed consisted of such legends as Andrea Martin, Eugene Levy, Martin Short, Joe Flaherty, Dave Thomas, and Catherine O'Hara. John Candy was most certainly there in spirit.

Again, any idiot, future or present, could have sold this show to the media. I was just happy to be in the room. As in I got to sit in the theater as they rehearsed and was ever so fortunate to get to watch the show. *SCTV* was my favorite TV show as a child. I got to the point in my media career of promoting something so hot that the size of it almost was a detriment to my future work. Soon after we made the announcement of the *SCTV* reunion show, a major media conglomerate that shall not be named swooped in and purchased media exclusivity for the event. Meaning all media attention was now to be exclusively distributed through its properties. As such, for the first time in my media career, I found myself having to refuse access to major outlets. It was very difficult having to say no to so many people in the media, especially those who had been so helpful to me along the way. Naturally, several of them were not too happy with me about it. It wasn't personal and so thankfully they got over it. Very big thank you to The Second City.

There are many names we could drop. However, it's not working for the big-name attractions that got us to this point. Again, it was supposed to be about us. What got us to this point was the countless small-room comedy shows, charity events, shows about former strippers finding Jesus, robots that enslave humans to perform rock music, indie pro-wrestling shows featuring zombies, pillow fight leagues, more comedy, gelato shops, mentalists, singing cowboys, street performers, independent authors, festivals, yoga classes for plus-sized women, children's theater, podcasts, Brazilian Capoeira, sumo wrestlers that now do comedy and only speak Japanese, national award shows, GASH, and countless sketch, stand-up, and improv comedy. These are the events that sculpted the information we've now passed on to you. Thank you to everyone who has ever asked for our help. And thanks to you for taking an interest; you now know as much as we do, so get out there and make amazing things happen. Come on! Git!

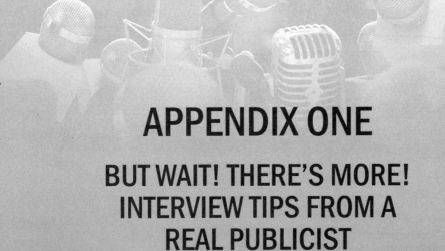

APPENDIX ONE

BUT WAIT! THERE'S MORE! INTERVIEW TIPS FROM A REAL PUBLICIST

When the good people of Self-Counsel Press opted to publish this mighty fine book, they sent me an information kit for authors. Within this information was a section about media for your book. It contained many helpful tips about conducting media interviews — a topic not originally covered in these pages. I thought to myself "This is really good — I'm totally stealing this for the book!"

Then it occurred to me that this is a publishing company with a real publicist. Would this publicist really be expected to pitch the media on a book encouraging people not to use publicists? This feels like the scene from the documentary *Roger & Me*, where we see an animatronic presentation of an auto worker serenading the robot that's taking his job. Also, how hypocritical and cowardly of me to have someone else do the publicity on this book. Have I always been such a monster?

Anyhow, Hanna Oliwa from Self-Counsel Press is a real, professional publicist. Her main objective is to obtain plenty of media attention for her clients, and not subtly manipulate the media to further her own creative agenda like some people we could mention. She has also not taken the premise of this book personally. Thank you, Hanna.

With that said, here are some really helpful interview tips, courtesy of Self-Counsel Press.

General Tips:

- Be yourself. Show the host or reporter and the audience who you are and why your project matters to you.

- Be confident. You were invited to an interview — that's a great achievement! The reporter or producer thinks you're a valuable source of information for his or her audience. Be confident about what you have to share.

- Be positive. Being interviewed can be stressful, especially if you've never done it before, but focusing on the positives will help you relax. Is the reporter fun to chat with? Is it your favorite radio program?

- Don't overpromote your product. It's understandable that you want to use this opportunity to promote yourself and your project, but think about what the audience is really looking for. They want information. A solution to a problem. Entertainment. How will your interview enrich their lives? Will you give them something to think about? Will it leave them with good — maybe even fun — associations with your name?

- Smile. It will put you in a better mood, the interviewer will perceive you as friendly, and so will the audience — even if it's a radio interview. Smiles can be heard!

More Practical Tips:

- Preparation is key. Know why you're there and what you're promoting. Have some important information and basic statistics on hand so you can illustrate the importance of your project.

- Decide on key points you'd like to make during the interview beforehand. This will give a structure to what you want to say, and it'll be easier to come up with answers if you stumble.

- This should go without saying, but here it is: Don't talk down to the interviewer or the audience. They want to learn something from you. Respect that.

- On radio/TV, maintain eye contact with the host. Read his or her body language. It will tell you if the host is interested in what you're talking about, and if he or she would like you to continue, or if he or she is about to interrupt.

- Be aware of the time. Before the interview, ask how long the segment is planned to be. During the interview — if possible — keep track of time so you can plan your answers and don't end up having to cram a lot of information into your last sentence.

Outlet-Specific Tips:

Radio

- Remember: The listeners will only hear your voice, so keep it interesting and engaging. If you're calling in, do it from a quiet place, with good reception. Hydrate to avoid cotton mouth!

TV

- Dress appropriately, preferably in dark and solid colors.

- Be mindful of your body language, keep your stance open and friendly. Sit up straight.

My Final Tip:

- Have fun! Promoting your project or business is not supposed to be a daunting task. You have something interesting to share with people, so go and show them why it's worth their while!

APPENDIX TWO

ADDITIONAL PRESS RELEASE SAMPLES

For immediate release – Oct 15, 2015
Please add to your listings and announcements

Crowdfunding Effort Seeks To Ensure Pillow Fight League's Triumphant Return

"A riot. Great fun for people who love action." — ESPN

(TORONTO — Oct. 15, 2015) One of the world's most original and engaging sports is poised to make a hell of a comeback. The Pillow Fight League ran from 2006 through 2011, hosting 65 events throughout North America until its ailing owner was forced to pull the plug due to health issues. Fortunately, 2015 saw Canadian media personality Brandy Dawley acquire the rights to the defunct league with the support of her ownership group. "I'm determined to not just return the PFL to its former glory, but to see it become bigger and better than ever before," says Dawley, who will serve as league president.

The PFL is excited to announce BringBackThePFL.com, an Indiegogo crowdfunding campaign geared at raising $20,000 for the league's relaunch. This figure will play a key role in offsetting initial operating costs, which include advertising and promotion, athlete compensation, insurance, staff, training, video production, and set / combat structure. Crowdfunders can claim prizes from official pillow cases to event tickets to behind-the-scenes access — all the way to being awarded their own private PFL event.

119

Dawley expects to meet and exceed the $20,000 total and usher in a new era for the PFL: "I intend to make the Pillow Fight League an internationally recognized name," she says. The league has already begun recruiting fighters, and if the campaign goes as planned, fans can expect its inaugural event to be staged this coming winter.

The Pillow Fight League (Hi-rez PFL photos here) isn't a series of cutesy slumber party fights, nor is it an entertainment entity with a predetermined outcome, as you'd find in professional wrestling. The fights are 100% authentic, and showcase a riveting combination of strategy, grace, and fierce aggression. The new league will feature an amended set of rules, many to be developed at an upcoming run of private exhibition matches. Plus, for the first time ever, fighters will now be assigned to specific weight classes — a decision that will only widen the sport's appeal.

Click below for the Indiegogo campaign video

A media phenomenon during its initial run, the Pillow Fight League garnered coverage from ESPN, *Good Morning America*, *Inside Edition*, ABC, NBC, CBS, FOX, MTV, VH1, *Sports Illustrated*, *Reader's Digest*, *The New York Times*, *The Washington Post*, *The Boston Herald*, *The National Enquirer*, *Maxim*, and many others. "The PFL is an intense and evolving fusion of culture, sport, and spectacle," Dawley explains. "And this crowdfunding campaign will play a huge role in spreading awareness of the amazing things to come."

Brandy Dawley Bio

Brandy Dawley is the President of the Pillow Fight League, having purchased the organization earlier this year. She was a proud supporter of the PFL from its earliest incarnation, and remains an outspoken, passionate champion of feminist ideology. A big fan of combat sports, Brandy intends to amass an army of strong, badass, unique female athletes to overthrow the current state of sports entertainment and make the PFL a household name. And with a solid team of fighters behind her, there's no doubt this powerhouse is a force to be reckoned with. With Brandy at the helm, the league will flourish like never before.

For interviews or additional information, please contact:
Daniel Shehori at Sweat Equity Publicity – (phone number here) (email address here)

For immediate release – Nov 6, 2013

Please add to your listings and announcements

The newest members of the Dark Horse Comics family are here to turn the zombie genre on its (severed) head with...

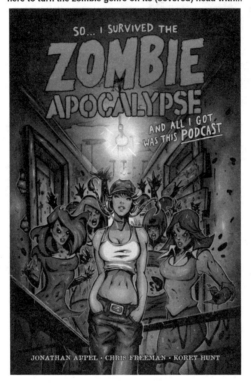

(LOS ANGELES — NOV 6, 2013) This November 20th, the legendary Dark Horse Comics will proudly release its genre-bending new graphic novel, *So... I Survived the Zombie Apocalypse and All I Got Was This Podcast*. And yep, this ain't your *father's* apocalypse: mostly because the planet's *males* may have been completely wiped out. Fortunately, women continue to thrive and survive — albeit as bloodthirsty zombies!

So... I Survived the Zombie Apocalypse was conceived and developed by Korey Hunt, screenwriter Chris Freeman, and writer/director Jonathan Appel. Following Appel's untimely death in 2010 at the age of 35, Hunt and Freeman teamed up with film producer friend Sarah Quay. Their goal: do everything possible to ensure Jonathan's vision might somehow see the light of day. Three years — and countless struggles — later, they've finally succeeded.

Mara Mitchell is humanity's lone, non-infected female in this edgy and comedic dystopian tale. She's young, idealistic, and beautifully geeky, with one heck of a podcast. And she's hell-bent on befriending her neighbors. One problem, though: the planet's zombie women turn out to be stone-cold catty! We're talking some serious undead 'tude! Can Mara charm her way into their cliquey decrepit girls club? Or will the unending rejection push our hero to the brink of an all-out war?

With its unique "females only" slant, *So... I Survived the Zombie Apocalypse* deliberately runs counter to what we've come to expect from the genre — a conceit Korey Hunt credits to the fertile mind of his late friend and writing partner. "Working with Jonathan was like trying to fill a bucket from a fire hose," says Hunt. "He would barrage you with ideas and you would just try to catch some of them, adding in your own when you had a minute to think."

As for future plans, Sarah Quay hopes a successful run will allow the creative team to "keep telling stories in this bizarre, clique-ish dystopia where the human male is endangered and Mara Mitchell may be his only hope." In the meantime, the group — collectively known as Slumber Vision — has already begun collaborating on a second book for Dark Horse Comics, titled, *Twinsburg*. Cocreator Chris Freeman describes it as "A murder mystery that takes place at a twins convention — with plenty of dark twists and turns, naturally."

Dark Horse Comics is one of the world's most respected publishers of graphic novels. Its licensed titles include comics based on *Star Wars*, *Avatar: The Last Airbender*, *Buffy the Vampire Slayer*, *Aliens*, *Predator*, and *Mass Effect*. Dark Horse also publishes creator-owned comics such as Frank Miller's *Sin City* and *300*, Mike Mignola's *Hellboy*, and Stan Sakai's *Usagi Yojimbo*.

So... I Survived the Zombie Apocalypse and All I Got Was This Podcast
Featuring animation by veteran illustrators Rich Bonk, Alan Kupperberg,
Jerry Beck, and Melike Acar
Available in all major North American comic stores on Nov 20, 2013
Also available for download internationally at www.digital.darkhorse.com

For interviews or additional information, please contact:
Daniel Shehori at Sweat Equity Publicity – (phone number here) (email address here)

For immediate release – August 9, 2016

Brickworks Entertainment presents...

(TORONTO — August 9, 2016) On Sunday, September 11, The Second City hosts a night of humor and storytelling from one of professional wrestling's most legendary — and infamous — figures. *An Evening With Jake "The Snake" Roberts* has the 6'6" Hall of Famer unleashing never-before-heard road stories from the WWE's most iconic era.

We're talking over-the-top tales of bouts, pranks, and locker room antics featuring everyone from Ravishing Rick Rude to Hacksaw Jim Duggan to the British Bulldogs to Andre the Giant to the Undertaker. A post-set Q&A will wrap up the evening, giving fans the chance to ask Jake anything they've ever wanted to know — no holds barred.

Click here for hi-rez photos of Jake

Bonus: the $30 VIP Fan Package includes one ticket, plus a meet & greet before the show, and a photo-op with Jake. The evening is hosted by David Andrew Brent, one of Canada's most talented comics and voice actors. Opening act is beloved stand-up veteran Mike Dambra. Whether you're a wrestling fan or not, Jake "The Snake" Roberts will keep you wrapped in his coils and leave you wanting more.

Jake's 2016 UnSpokeN WorD TouR comes on the heels of the critically acclaimed *The Resurrection of Jake the Snake Roberts*. The gripping documentary (now on Netflix) chronicled the wrestling superstar's battles with past demons as he struggled to reclaim his life and the family that gave up on him.

An Evening With Jake "The Snake" Roberts

The Second City

51 Mercer St., Toronto

Sunday, September 11, 2016

Doors at 9pm, show at 10pm

Advance Tickets: $30.00 at www.SecondCity.com/Shows/Toronto

Remaining tickets (if available) at the door

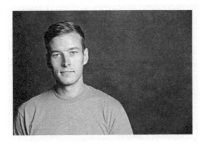

David Andrew Brent (Host) One of Canada's most talented and diverse voice actors, impressionists, and stand-up comedians, David Andrew Brent has worked exclusively with many of the world's best talent. Opening for the likes Jim Jefferies, Anthony Jeselnik, the Trailer Park Boys and many more, David has become a staple in the Canadian Comedy scene.

Mike Dambra (Opening Act) Involved in the comedy scene since 1986, Mike has become a comedy staple and a club favorite. In 1987 and 1997 he claimed the "Funniest Person In Rochester" title. Armed with the ability to adapt to any audience, Mike has the willingness to offer up brutal truths and unforgiving views. Mike has toured with such acts as Rosie O'Donnell, Adam Sandler, Michael Bolton, and Joan Jett & The Blackhearts. His own headlining shows continue to earn rave reviews across North America.

For interviews or additional information, please contact:
Daniel Shehori at Sweat Equity Publicity – (phone number here) (email address here)

TORONTO

APPENDIX THREE

SPONSORSHIP LETTER TEMPLATE

SPONSORSHIP LETTER TEMPLATE

[RECIPIENT NAME]
[RECIPIENT TITLE]
[RECIPIENT ORGANIZATION]
[RECIPIENT ADDRESS]

Begin below if your correspondence is by email and not traditional mail.

Dear [RECIPIENT NAME],

My name is [NAME]. As an admirer of your organization, I'm asking that you consider becoming a corporate sponsor for [YOUR THING].

[DESCRIPTION OF YOUR THING]

Make the description brief, punchy, and exciting, without being too "salesy." Explain why you strongly believe it will be a success.

[YOUR THING] offers three levels of sponsorship, each of which provide significant exposure:

Amend these sponsorship levels to your specifications.

- Silver — $[LOWER AMOUNT]. Your company name/logo appears in all printed material, including posters, banners, and our website. It will also be promoted through our social media channels.

- Gold — $[LARGER AMOUNT]. The above benefits are included, plus [ADDITIONAL BENEFITS].

- Platinum — $[HIGHEST AMOUNT]. All above benefits are included, plus your organization will be listed as our primary sponsor in all promotional material, media interviews, and social media channels.

My hope is that your organization will take interest in joining [MY THING] at one of these sponsorship levels. I've attached my [THING] fact sheet, which provides more detailed information. Please feel free to contact me with any questions or clarifications. I'm excited at the prospect of working with you, and I look forward to speaking with you at your earliest convenience.

Best regards,

[YOUR NAME AND TITLE]
[YOUR PHONE NUMBER AND EMAIL]
[LINK(S) TO YOUR SOCIAL MEDIA PAGE(S) OR WEBSITE]

Attach a brief fact sheet, or at the very least, your press release.